I'm Still Standing

"Crawling out of darkness to stand in the Light"

By

Mildred D. Muhammad

This book is dedicated to those who don't believe they can heal from the pain of abuse. Although the journey will be long and painful, you can survive, heal and thrive. Don't allow anyone to tell you that you can't.

"Release your faith,
knowing with assurance,
that **ALL** circumstances
will work in
YOUR
favor today!"

~ Mildred D. Muhammad ~

Table of Contents

Foreward *13*

Chapter 1
The Isolation 17

Chapter 2
The Execution 25

Chapter 3
Aftermath 39

Chapter 4
Overcoming Difficulties 49

Chapter 5
Having Faith in The Process 59

Chapter 6
Creating a New "*Normal*" 83

Chapter 7
Healing & Moving Forward 105

Afterword *115*

ACKNOWLEDGMENTS

I thank Almighty God Allah, for giving me the strength, comfort, confidence and love that has and continues to propel me throughout my life's' journey.

To my children, John, Salena and Taalibah, who love, support and encourage me. All of you are the wind beneath my wings. Every time I look at your faces and hear your voices, all of you remind me that the promises of God are true! He promised that you would be returned to me and here you are! I love you all so very much.

To my family and friends, in person and on social media, thank you for pouring your love, inspirational messages and songs, into my spirit throughout my journey. You are an everyday blessing to me. I love and appreciate each one of you!

MILDRED D. MUHAMMAD

FOREWORD

November 10, 2009 was the day that the man who fathered my children was executed. He was a father, my ex-husband and who the world knew as *"The D.C. Sniper."*

I never thought that John would be executed. With so many people on death row, I thought that it would take years for his execution to happen. With his appeals and constantly fighting for a new trial, it didn't occur to me that the execution would be carried out so soon after his conviction.

On September 9, 2009, the prosecutor sent a letter to Prince William Circuit Court in Manassas, requesting an execution date for November 9th. The Senior Assistant Attorney General, Katherine B. Burnett, wrote that the November 9th date had been coordinated with the governor's office to ensure consideration of an expected clemency petition. The date was changed to November 10th, the day before Veteran's Day.

It was clear to me, that although the wheels of justice had been turning slowly, for so long, it felt like they had kicked into full throttle. When the reality of the execution finally set in, the only people I thought about were my children.

I knew the time had come for their dad's life to come to an end. He was going to be executed.

Prior to the trial, law enforcement had informed me that I was the intended target. They said that John created a diversion, by killing innocent people to cover up my murder so he could come in as the grieving father and gain custody of our children. One of the agents said, *"we asked John why did he do it"?* John replied, *"Its Mildred's fault"*. He asked, *"why would he say that?"* I said, *"I don't know. I just asked him for a divorce"*. He's blaming me for his actions. That was a hard pill to swallow. I thought of the family members of the people he killed. My heart went out to them and my heart ached as well.

I was experiencing both mixed and unexplainable emotions. It was hard for me to comprehend what I was feeling. The life that I had been living, moving on, and trying to be a good mother, would not have been a reality, had John been able to accomplish killing me. I wondered where my children would have ended up.

When I learned that John was going to be executed, I worried about my children's fears and what they were feeling. *How could I help my children get through this unusual situation? What could I say to them that would ease their minds and soothe their injured spirits?*

They were young and deserved to have a normal, peaceful life. That would not be the case. Unfortunately, their minds were heavy with thoughts of growing up without a mother and father at home to protect them, keep them safe and ensure that their home would be filled with love, like children who were their age. But I had already come to accept that was not our fate. Still, I wanted to protect my children from what was to come. The feelings and emotions that I was experiencing were new to me and required total examination.

This was uncharted territory for all of us. I was aware that my children and I would be in situations that we should not have to face. It was important to me that I stay emotionally connected to them. Regardless of whom or what, my children are always my priority! I continued to build up my faith and strength for them. We were **NOT** going to be held accountable for John's actions.

"My prayer, my sacrifice, my life and my death are all

for Allah, the Lord of the Worlds. No associate has He and this I am commanded and I am of those who submit."

This was a portion of a prayer I prayed as a reminder that Allah is always with me. I asked Him to give me strength and wisdom to make the right decisions for us regarding John's execution. I asked Him to help me protect my children. I truly believe that He gave me exactly what I asked for on that day, just like He had given me the strength and endurance to handle the days preceding November 10, 2009. The portal to healing seemed hard to find, but recovery from the distressing darkness was ultimately there. I knew I would rise in the light again. I became strong because my faith was stronger.

Reading Psalms 91 helped me tremendously. Psalms 91 is referred to as *"the survivor's scripture"*. I believe it is called that because the scripture speaks of the ways God will protect those who call upon Him. The part of the scripture that resonated with my spirit, throughout the whole ordeal were of the last three versus. I changed the pronouns (*you* to *me, you* to *I, your* to *my, him* to *her*) because I needed to feel that Allah was talking to me. I needed to feel His protective arms around me to get through this awful time with my children.

It reads:

14 "Because he (*she*) loves me," says the LORD, "I will rescue   him (*her*);

I will protect him(*her*), for he(*she*) acknowledges my name.

15 He (*She*) will call on me, and I will answer him (*her*);

I will be with him (*her*) in trouble,

I will deliver him (*her*) and honor him (*her*).

16 With long life will I satisfy him (*her*) and show him *(her)* my salvation."

15

My prayer and verses 14-16 sustained me. Allah allowed the words to be the pathway for me as I went through the healing portal and to keep moving on through to the other side. When I'm troubled, I concentrate on my prayers and these verses. Today, I recite the entire scripture every morning after saying my prayers.

By Allah's grace and mercy, I was assured that my children and I were not alone.

I've dedicated my life to helping survivors and victims of domestic abuse and domestic violence. Using my story to inspire others who have been through the turmoil of domestic violence, abuse and living in fear, has helped bring peace, not only to the lives of those I help, but to my life as well. I have gone beyond surviving. I was a victim, who became a survivor and a warrior on these issues and I've moved on to being…a THRIVER!

There were times when I felt isolated, unsure and afraid. Isolation was paralyzing because it made me feel trapped inside of myself. I withdrew from others and stayed within. At first, I felt like it was a safe and secure place…it wasn't. Isolation made me feel more alone and lost in the darkness of my situation. The immobilizing feeling made me feel no one cared. The weight of my situation knocked me down and further away from the light. That was then…no longer do I feel this way.

A few more years would pass before I would find the power and strength to share my story. My children are my motivation to move forward and continue this journey beyond surviving. Allah and my children are the reasons why

I'm Still Standing!

CHAPTER 1

THE ISOLATION

Being free of the abuse and fear that John brought into my life, did not mean that I was free from the aftermath of all the events that had occurred. The life that I am living now is not the life I would be living had John been able to kill me. My children would have had to live their lives without their mother.

Although I had come to accept that John had stopped loving me a long time ago, I had been puzzled as to why he wanted to kill me. His level of hatred was deeper than I had ever imagined. It used to hurt me whenever I thought of how much he hated me. He had told me that I had become his enemy. As his enemy, he felt I had to die. It was not clear to me how I had become his enemy and what I had done to drive him to the point of wanting to take my life.

Despite John's efforts to take away my joy and healing, I was not going to allow him to win. I had an internal struggle that I knew I had to get through. It was important that I move forward not only for myself, but for my children. I would be forced to emotionally fight this battle alone.

And in fact, I found myself alone. I asked myself, *"Who can I actually talk to? Who can I really confide in? Where can I find genuine comfort?"* Of course, my children would have all the comfort and confidence that they needed from me. However, given the circumstances, I could not immediately find the answers to the questions that I asked myself.

John's story was sensationalized. The news about his history in the military, his crimes, his conviction, our children and some parts of our relationship was everywhere. The media seemed to spread certain details and opinions about us. Everyone knew about John from his past to the present. They knew about the people that he shot and killed, their families and how he carried out one of the most horrendous crimes of the century. It seemed they knew all about John and the stories of his victims and their families.

The truth about me and my children was not being reported. The media knew the truth, but did not report it. John secured the ratings for their network, not the abuse me and my children went through. There was no emphasis on the time when I had to run for my life nor how for 18 months, I struggled and fought to find my children. No reports about the pain and horror that my children suffered while in Antiqua.

Yes, prior to all the terror, John had been a good father and husband. He was once a man that I had loved. Suddenly, that man did not exist anymore. The man who I looked to always love me in return, had removed himself from my life. In his words, I had become his enemy. A man that I once loved wanted to take my life. I was a victim. My children were taken away to make me come back to him. Yes, children are used as pawns in abusive relationships. When I did not conform to his wishes, he decided that I didn't deserve to live.

A victim is often looked upon as a person who has been physically harmed, sexually assaulted, mutilated, or even killed. Some people form an opinion about what a victim should be from reality shows and reports they watch on television or the tragic, heart wrenching stories they read in newspapers and magazines or someone who has suffered physical injuries as a result of a blatant crime or horrible accident. However, 80% of victims of domestic abuse/violence do not have physical scars to prove they are victimized. Therefore, it makes it difficult for the victims and survivors, who have the deepest-rooted emotional scars, to be taken seriously. Then what are we supposed to do?

I felt I had a double-edged sword held against my throat. I didn't know John was the sniper until the police told me. I was looking for the profile that was given to us by the FBI profilers, just like everyone else. I wanted law enforcement to tell everyone what they told me, that I was the target! I thought, if I spoke out, I would have been seen as a liar, as victims are often viewed. However, if I did not speak up, I would have eventually lost my life. Had I been killed, perhaps people I once knew would have held vigils and told the media about how I was a good person and I had seemed to be generous and kind. But where were those caring people when I had reached out for help?

I was between a rock and a hard place, not knowing which way to turn. That place located between the rock and the hard place was my isolation. I allowed myself to stay in that rough space. I was waiting for a portal to open so I could be taken somewhere else.

Isolation is a dark and lonely place. It doesn't just happen. One does not suddenly decide to cut off their friends and associates. No, isolation is a deserted feeling that builds up slowly from the inside. Eventually, the loneliness eats away the fear and shameful feelings that one may have felt. With isolation comes depression. It can cut you off from people who are important in your life as well as those whom you may feel have contributed to the depression. Isolation has layers that continues to pile up over you, until you're surrounded by your own thick, dark walls. There, you feel as if no one can get to you. You feel somewhat protected from what you were once ashamed and afraid of.

Eventually, I welcomed being alone. It was shortly after people noticed me as John's ex-wife. They needed someone to the blame. They chose me because John was not available. I was an easy target.

I was told that I took away the peace from this quiet

community. I was to blame for the death of many people. Some in the community said to me, *"Had I stayed with him, he would have just killed me"*. Another comment, *"If I would have stayed on the west coast, the people on the east coast would still be alive"*. People spoke their feelings to me and how I contributed to the chaos John had caused. Some people even blamed me directly to my face. But I took it. I did not debate with anyone about the crime John committed. They needed someone to blame and unfortunately, it was me.

The media knew how to sensationalize and create theories about every part of the story. They even blamed me by picking apart my restraining order and telling me what I should or should not have done. I was blamed by so many people and very few wanted to be seen with me.

I couldn't go to the store to buy groceries without being bashed with unkind words from strangers. I tried to dress differently by changing my wardrobe. I even tried to dress down and poorly, in a manner that I normally wouldn't go out of the house. It didn't seem to make a difference because people would still recognize me. It became difficult to protect my children from what was being said. I knew that I had to do, everything in my power, to keep people from hurting them.

I began planning my errands when I knew people would be at work. I limited my activities to only going to work and then coming right back home. If I felt the need to go outside, I would sit in the chair in my backyard where I knew no one would bother me. I tried not to go anywhere that I did not have to go. Rationing my time became easy after a while because the less time I had to spend outside of my home, the less time I would have to spend trying to protect myself and my children.

After all the abusive words, lack of compassion and mistreatment from people that I thought would understand, I allowed the isolation to become my friend. The isolation kept me safe and I embraced it.

People that I knew, both friends and associates, tried to be there for me and my children, but I wanted to avoid any new hindrances that could have driven the wedges between us any deeper. They meant well, but I understood that they were limited to their own experiences and circumstances. I couldn't have expected them to come close to understanding all that we had been through. *How could they understand something so tragic without experiencing it for themselves when I was having issues with it as well?* Our struggles were not your everyday family issues. Tragically, this was life and death for us.

In a way, I felt I had been protecting the few friends that I had by pushing them away. By the time I had become used to isolating myself, those friends were long gone. There were a couple of friends who tried to get through to me, but I rejected their sincerity. I chose not to confide in any of my friends because if the media, police, or any of the others who were against me tried to question them, then they could honestly say that they didn't know anything.

I tried to explain my emotions, but no one seemed to understand. I just prayed that no one I cared about would ever experience this feeling of isolation that my children and I had come to accept.

Somehow, I had convinced myself that I was not hurting anyone by choosing to isolate myself. Besides, I was used to being alone from the time I had to hide in the shelter, changed my name, and give up my identity from the very moment when reality struck me. Some of the people I wanted to trust had become intolerant and uncaring towards me and my children.

What was I supposed to do to protect myself and my children? How could I protect my children from criticism and judgment? I decided to disconnect from everyone and everything. I convinced myself that this was the best thing to do. But, after a while, it became difficult for me to connect to other people's feelings, actions and behaviors. I did not give the emotional reactions that people wanted from me. I detached from their emotions. I built a wall to protect us. Within those walls, I created my life.

I had decided that I would not unload my burdens on anyone accept Allah. He had blessed me with the ability to write out my thoughts and feelings. Journaling was a safe haven for me within my isolated walls. It became a way for me to search deep inside of myself for the answers to the questions that I had once asked myself and couldn't seem to find the answers. Journaling allowed me to open up without fear of judgment and rejection. I did not have to second guess myself by wondering if what I was doing was right or wrong. Through journaling, I confronted every thought and emotion that I would not speak aloud to anyone, except God.

Writing out my deepest, darkest emotions allowed me to understand who I had been and who I was becoming. Writing played a huge part in my healing process. I was able to encourage myself, build myself up and through prayer and gaining knowledge from God's word, I was made strong. I knew I was not alone. The journey that I had to go through, to become more aware of who I am and where I was going, was with Allah. I was finding myself as I was traveling through a portal of healing.

As I began to allow myself to heal and open spiritually, I knew of one person who would accept me for who I am and not judge my emotions and that is my sister/friend, Olivia. Even though she's 3000 miles away, she did not let the distance stop her from being my friend. She knew the danger I had faced with John because he threatened to kill her too. Even before this started, she asked did I realize I was sleeping with a trained killer. At that time, I didn't think anything of it because I felt he would not do anything to hurt me.

I told her that it seemed as if people were afraid to be near me. Olivia encouraged me to stop isolating myself. I felt that she would not have a reason to give me wrong advice. After all, she had been my friend even when I had tried to push her away. I thank Allah every day for Olivia and her loving patience and support. I view her as my sister, not my friend. And to this day, we continue to communicate.

Who would have thought that I could help others by sharing my story with them? How was it possible for me to help other people when it seemed like they were against me? Everything was about understanding what the "D.C. Sniper" did and why he did it!

Unfortunately, I and my children weren't seen or treated as victims. And with all that we had been through, now it was time to face the execution.

MILDRED D. MUHAMMAD

CHAPTER 2

THE EXECUTION

John used to say: *"If you're man enough to do the crime, then be man enough to do the time...whatever that may be."*

In April of 2005, John was found guilty and given the death penalty. The ruling for his execution had been affirmed by the Virginia Supreme Court. It was stated that John could be sentenced to death because the sniper murders were seen as part of an act of terrorism. John continued to fight.

John's lawyers were doing everything in their power to try to get him clemency. His lawyers argued that he had not been the one who committed the murders, he was not the triggerman. They argued that it was his younger partner, Lee Boyd Malvo. The boy that John had originally sent to my front door to kill me. The defense had been hoping to get John life without parole.

It seemed very odd to me that John was fighting to avoid the death penalty when he had taken the lives of so many innocent people. He had been found guilty and sentenced. Yet, John was not willing to do the time to pay for his crimes because he wanted to keep fighting. A walking contradiction to the man who once said that a guilty man should take responsibility for his criminal actions.

I was at work when I found out that John was going to be executed. I immediately thought about my children. John was away in college and my girls were in high school.

I asked myself, *"How are my children going to handle this? What will I tell them? What will they say? How will they react?"* With so many questions running through my mind, I needed to find the answers before they found out about their dad from someone else. I was fearful that they would find out through the media or other people who were talking about it and I wouldn't be there, at the moment, they found out. I wanted to be there for them.

Since I was at work, I put in a request to get off early. My employer understood my circumstances and granted permission. I rushed home so I could be the one to tell them about their dad's sentence.

We did not expect John's execution to be decided and announced so soon. I had not been prepared to have to tell them that day and to be honest, I don't think I would have been prepared on any day.

John was in his sophomore year at Louisiana Tech. As soon as I arrived home, I called him. As the phone rang, *I wondered if he had heard? What must John be feeling or thinking at that moment?* He finally picked up.

"Hi Mom," he said. He sounded like himself. It didn't seem like he knew anything about his dad's situation.

"Hey honey. Did you hear about your dad's sentence?" I calmly asked John.

John simply said, *"No",* and then became very silent.

I took a slow, deep breath and told him what had been decided.

"He was found guilty and given the death penalty," I said.

Still, John remained silent. No verbal reaction came from his end. Not a sound.

"John, I know that it is a lot to take in."

He suddenly said, *"That's kind of fast, isn't it?"*

I responded, *"Compared to most cases, yes, it does seem quick. My understanding is that your dad has exhausted all his appeals for a new trial. He hasn't been granted a new one. Therefore, they had to take the next step. The request for an execution date must go in. That is where they are right now. There's nothing else that he can do."*

I couldn't see his face to know if he was alright. His silence bothered me. Like my daughters, I wanted John to be safe at home with me when finding out about this news.

I asked, *"Would you like to come home and be with us right now?"*

I could hear the hesitation in his voice as he began to answer. I could tell he wanted to handle this on his own.

He said, *"It's okay, mom. I have support here. My frat brothers know who my dad is. I think that I will be okay if I just stay at school."*

John was grown up enough to know what he needed. Fortunately, he had the support of his fraternity brothers. It was comforting to know that he was not alone. His friends knew who his dad was. They knew what he had been through and they gave him the kind of support that a caring family would give to their loved one. He felt that when he told his friends about his dad's execution and how soon it was happening, they would support him. It put my mind at ease to know that he was surrounded by his other family. For the time being, I let it go.

To be pro-active, I contacted Louisiana Tech administrative offices. I spoke with one of deans. I told him who I was and that my son is in their school. I told him that I needed them to know what was happening so my son would be protected. He thanked me for calling and appreciated me thinking of them in this time. I told him it was only fair that I inform them of the situation so they could prepare themselves. He said he would ensure his safety and to keep in touch. I felt better after that conversation.

Salena and Taalibah were attending Suitland High School. Despite my efforts to tell them of the verdict myself, unfortunately, my girls had heard the news. They ran to me to ask if I knew about their dad. Taalibah was anxious. She approached me with Salena by her side.

"Mom, did you hear the news?" Taalibah asked.

Salena said, *"They are going to execute Dad in November!"*

My only response was, *"Yes, honey. I heard."*

"That's kind of quick, isn't it?" she asked.

I explained to them the circumstances surrounding their dad's appeals and the process that the lawyers were in. Their facial expressions seemed to change. Their faces looked heavy with sadness and worry. All they could seem to do is stare at me in disbelief. I continued to explain the process to them, as I had done with John, so that they could understand.

It was a struggle to find the right words to ease their minds. However, nothing came to me. All the explaining in the world not have made a difference. At the time, the only thing that I could do was hold them.

I had to continue to find ways for them to cope with their dad's sentence. It wouldn't be easy for them, but I wanted them to know that I was doing everything that I could to give them support. My efforts were to keep their minds, spirits and hearts at ease and to help them through this tragically extraordinary situation.

It was at this time that my children expressed their desire to speak with their dad. I had to consider the process of making that happen for them.

I felt uneasy to know that my children could get a chance to talk to their dad. John had the power to unravel the efforts I put into helping them to heal from the trauma they experienced. He would have manipulated everything I had done with his usage of words.

It took an insurmountable amount of time and energy to help my children cope and heal from the psychological damage that had resulted from being with John in those 18 months. I did not want all the work we had put into healing, mentally and psychologically, to go to waste. My job was to be pro-active in their lives and guide them, despite the crimes their dad had committed. I had to face this life changing decision. The wrong decision could ruin their lives. I was certain that if I had not allowed them to talk to their dad before he died, they would have held it against me forever. I feared that they would have hated me. As I had always done, I put my trust and faith in God and let him guide me.

Surprisingly, I had received a victim's package in the mail. It arrived by way of the Attorney General's Office. The package explained what was required of the victims of the offender. It stated the "dos and don'ts" for victims in this kind of situation. The package included the information pertaining to John's execution - what was granted and permitted to do.

A few days later, the Attorney General's office called. I thought that they were calling to update me on John's status or give me information about when my children will be able to speak with their dad. It was not at all what I had expected.

The reason for the call was to apologize for sending me the information regarding the victim's package. Per the State of Virginia, my children and I were not considered John's victims. By their definition, victims included the families and survivors of John's D.C. Sniper rampage.

Suddenly, I had been reminded of the insensitivity I had experienced during this whole ordeal. The pain came back all over again. It was a shock to hear the words spoken out loud.

Their representative confirmed what I had known all along. My children and I had not been thought of nor taken into consideration during that time pending John's execution. But I had already come to accept that this was how we were going to be treated. I was right on track with how I had felt because of the way we were treated. Because it was a *'family matter'*, courts view family issues differently than other courts. It felt like everything John had done to us was legal. No consequences for his actions. Everything outside of *'us'* was illegal. I wanted and needed justice for what he did to us.

I had spoken to a colleague, Anne Seymour, and told her that the Attorney General Office did not consider me or my children to be victims so they would not let us know anything about his court proceedings or any other information regarding his trial. She was saddened to hear that and encouraged me to sign up with VINE, the national victim's notification network. VINE stands for Victim Information and Notification Everyday. This service allows crime victims to obtain timely and reliable information about criminal cases and the custody status of offenders 24 hours a day. VINE allows victims to call to inquire about the current status of an offender and register to be notified immediately in the event of an offender's release, escape, transfer and court appearance.

VINE is accessible via the internet through their website, (https://www.vinelink.com), and on the VINE mobile app that was made for mobile devices.

VINE is located in the area where we lived. So, I signed up. This was a useful way for us to keep up with the latest news on John's status.

In mid-October, I brought John home from college. He had the friendship and support of administrative staff, fraternity brothers and associates at school, but it was time for him to be home with his family. He needed to be home. A legal execution is an unusual way for a parent to die and it would be difficult for them to handle the death of their dad in this way.

Despite it all, it still hurt them to know that their dad was going to be executed. John had committed terrible, unexplainable, traumatically, devastating crimes. He changed the lives of many with his horrific behavior and actions, including his own children. My children had been faced with all of these things and knew that the consequences for their dad's crimes was death. Now, all they wanted to do was talk to him before he would be executed.

John's attorney gave me direct instructions on the process to manually go about putting in a request for my children to speak with their father. It would involve putting in a request and John approving our request.

I was to contact the warden's office. From there, John would be notified to put John, Salena and Taalibah's names on the docket as his visitors. Once John had placed their names on his roster, then we would receive notification through my attorney. We had followed the instructions accordingly and hoped for the best. They looked to me for strength. My strength came from Allah.

They were going to have their time to speak to their dad. They were going to have their opportunity to say their goodbyes and ask the burning question that John would finally have to answer – *Why?*

While I waited for a confirmation that my children would get to speak to their dad, I kept my faith in Allah. I had faith that He would help me to be strong for my children. I didn't feel any emotions. It was not obvious to anyone, including my children. My focus was on them. I thought of their suffering. *How could I help them get through their dad's execution and maintain their sanity?*

A month had passed. It was November 8, 2009, two days before John was scheduled to be executed, and we still had not received a phone call from John. John's attorney had been working to get him clemency. Still, they were hoping to get John life without the possibility of parole.

Protestors were starting to speak out about the death penalty. People had their own opinions. Most of the nation was for John's execution. Other people were against it. They called the execution, inhumane. Some people felt hope.

My children were on an emotional roller coaster because they wanted to talk to their dad. They were clear and open with their feelings. It was hard on them to know that their dad was going to die, but they were more concerned with having a chance to say goodbye to him. They had accepted the decision of the court.

People wanted to know my personal stance on the execution. I told my children that whatever the jury decided, that is what we would accept. That was my stance on this case. Every action I took was for them. My only thoughts were about them and how they were feeling. I was concerned about their mental stability and emotional well-being. If it were not for my children, I don't think that I would've paid much attention to the process.

I chose to settle with the facts. I was not allowing myself to become emotionally attached to the issue. I had been so far removed, emotionally, from this situation. The closer it came to the time for the execution, the more detached I felt from the process.

I had already grieved over our relationship. It was over a long time before that day. John hated me. He wanted to kill me. He took my children away. And even now, he seemed to want to deny our children of the last chance they'd have to talk to him and finalize making their peace with this whole ordeal.

Why should I have felt any emotion for him?

What mattered the most to me, was the fact that my children anxiously waited for some form of correspondence from their dad.

The warden responded by saying that John would not cooperate. He would not put the children's names on the dockets therefore they would not be allowed to see him. I thanked him for responding. I told my children the information the warden told me. They were angry and John asked, *'what's up with that Mom"? Why would dad not want to see us? He said he took us because he loved us. This isn't love to me.* I didn't say anything.

November 10th, the day John was scheduled to be executed, had arrived. John, Salena and Taalibah stayed home. They did not want to be around anyone that day. It was important to them that all of us stay together for emotional support. No one else was invited to be with us because I did not want my children to feel like they couldn't grieve in their own way. They did not have to feel like they had to hold back in expressing their emotions in fear of how others would react to them. It was their time to grieve freely and openly.

We turned on CNN. My son had been crying the night before, and by now, I could tell that he was exhausted. Taalibah and Salena sat quietly with tears in their eyes.

My heart was breaking for my children. It was painful to see them cry. I needed to be strong for them.

Taalibah cried, *"Ma, this is it! Can we please talk to dad? We have not had a chance to talk to him since he's been in prison. He's going to die today. Mom, please!"*

Salena watched with curiosity, tears flowing.

"We won't ever have a chance to talk to him again, Mom!" John pleaded.

Since they were unable to see him, they settled for a phone call that was to come from his attorney with John on the phone. *"It's not going to be long,"* I tried to reassure them. *"The attorney said to stay by the phone. He said that we should receive a call right before he goes in."*

My words only seemed to make them more anxious. I could only tell them what I had been told. It seemed as if they knew what I had felt.

CNN announced the names of the people who John was going to see and talk to before his scheduled execution. My children listened again with hope, but still, there names were not mentioned. That is when their tears dried up and their emotions turned into anger.

John turned to me, fueling with anger, *"Mom? What does that mean?"* John asked. *"What's up with that, Mom? Why is dad doing this to us? Why won't he talk to us?"*

I didn't know the answer to his questions. Only John could provide the answers. They had every right to be angry and ask their questions. There were a lot of questions that would remain unanswered for a long time. I stayed quiet and let them talk out their anger and pain.

Taalibah sobbed, *"What did we do? This isn't fair! He said that he kidnapped us because he loved us. If he loves us, why won't he talk to us? Why, Mom?"*

John shook his head as if he was trying to shake away the anger. The more he thought about it, the angrier he seemed to become.

"That's not love!" John shouted before storming out of the room.

I followed John, leaving Taalibah and Salena in the living room together. He stomped down the hallway. I calmly reached out to him. I could feel my son's anger radiating from his body. Knowing that I was behind him, John stopped and turned to me. He immediately seemed to calm down when I touched him.

"I'm good, Mom," he took a deep breath and said. *"I just really need to be alone right now. Please, can I be alone?"*

I nodded. There were no words. I was so much concern for my children. They had to be allowed to grieve in their own way because they had the right to do so. No matter how hard it was for me, I had to respect their boundaries.

As evening approached, they grew even more anxious. They still had 'hope' that their dad would call. Their anxiety and cries pushed me to call John's attorney again. There was no answer. I encouraged them to try to be patient and have faith that God will allow the best outcome for them. John's attorney said that he would do everything that he could so that they would be able to talk to John before it was too late. They seemed to calm down for a while as we waited for the phone to ring and continued to watch the clock.

Salena, Taalibah and I continued to watch CNN to see if there were any new developments. John joined us after he had taken some time to be alone. They continued to wait for a phone call from John's attorney.

Not long after nightfall, we noticed a man walking up

to the podium on the television. The man seemed to take his time. He walked very slowly with his head down. His demeanor was somber. He scuffled and moved slowly while he prepared to speak. I knew that it had been done. John was dead. I watched my children's faces.

"John Allen Muhammad was pronounced dead at 9:11pm," he announced. John chose not to allow his children to speak to him before his execution. He denied them the chance to say goodbye.

Without another word, John left the room. Taalibah dropped to the floor and began screaming uncontrollably. Salena sat on the sofa. She sobbed quietly. All three of my children were on different levels of emotion.

First, I went to my son. I wanted to comfort him. I found him sitting in the living room. He sat quietly in the dark. I didn't exactly know what to say to him. I couldn't think of anything that would seem like the right words to bring him comfort. I stood silently and watched him. I waited for him to open up and speak.

He said, *"Mom, I'm good."*

I said, "okay honey". I turned and walked away.

Again, it was hard for me, but I had to give him his space. I went back to Salena and Taalibah. Salena sat on the sofa as she sobbed softly. Taalibah continued to moan and cry on the floor. I sat next to her and scooped her into my arms. I cradled her like I used to hold her when she was a baby.

It was heart wrenching to hear her cry out in so much emotional pain. I could hear the disappointment and anger in her screams. I just continued to hold her so that she could feel comforted by me as she released her grief. Taalibah looked up at me as I held her. Her eyes seemed to search mine for some kind of emotions. She seemed to want to see my reaction to her dad's execution. I did not have any feelings. There were no emotions from me regarding John.

In that moment, all I could think about was the agony my children were in. This was the result of John's actions.

This was the way his children would remember him. The time they needed to talk to him the most, he disappointed them tremendously.

Taalibah saw that there was no compassion. I had let John go a long time ago. I severed every emotional tie I had to him.

When Taalibah looked into my eyes and saw nothing, she stopped crying. She stood up, wiped her tears and walked away.

I said, *"are you okay honey?* She said, *I'm good."*

My oldest daughter, Salena continued to sob as she sat on the sofa. I went over to her to see if there was any way I could bring some comfort to her. She saw me coming towards her and lifted her head towards me. She didn't want to be held.

Angrily, she shouted, *"I hate him!"*

I said to Salena, *"No, you don't hate your dad."*

"Yes, I do," she said.

"You're just angry at him", I said.

"Don't tell me how I feel! I am angry and I hate him! You don't understand. He was going to kill you, Mom! He was going to leave us without a Mother. How could he say he loves us and he was going to kill you?"

There was nothing more that I could say. My children had to grieve in their own way. I respected their feelings.

I couldn't understand why John had refused to call and speak with them. I couldn't comprehend why he would deny his children the chance to say goodbye.

John's attorney finally got in touch with me. He told me what John said regarding why he would not call.

He said it was because of his shame for what he had done and his fear of me. He said John hated me. He said, "if John had chosen to speak with John, Salena and Taalibah, he wouldn't have been able to answer them when they would have asked him why. Answering their questions would have unraveled all the work he had put into his preparation for the execution". I told my children the response of John's attorney. They said that excuse was unacceptable.

John stayed true to the man that I knew he was. He didn't make a final statement before he was given the lethal injection. He wasn't going to say anything that would be analyzed and dissected. He didn't want anyone to try to find any kind of meaning or reasoning in his words. Therefore, he chose to remain silent. John did not apologize to anyone. He maintained his innocence until his final breath.

My children and I stayed together that evening. I had been emotionless for so long. My children needed me to help them through their grieving. I was able to handle my responsibility to my children. I listened to their cries. I held them in my arms and let them express their grief in the way that they needed to grieve. I provided comfort with coping techniques and healing from this trauma.

The pain of this tragedy was not close to being over. Although the execution was done, we still had to deal with the aftermath.

MILDRED D. MUHAMMAD

CHAPTER 3

THE AFTERMATH

The execution had passed. Before John was put to death, he had chosen not to talk to our children. Because he had made this decision, John, Salena and Taalibah, were left with the pain of not being able to say goodbye.

The next morning, they asked me if they could attend their dad's funeral. I felt torn. On one hand, I understood that they had to find peace within themselves. Since they did not speak to him, it seemed like it would be fair to let them go to his funeral so that they could find closure. On the other hand, I did not want them to face the public and the media after everything that they had been through.

After all the adversity and turmoil that we had overcome and had begun to heal from, I wondered, when would I be released from having to make these tough decisions?

After a few days of contemplation, deep meditation and prayer, I decided to take them to Louisiana, to go to John's funeral. We traveled to Baton Rouge, Louisiana on November 16th. It was one day before John's funeral.

The media was on top of the story about his execution, his funeral, me and our children. There was a lot of talk going around about John's funeral. They found out John had written letters to his children and others. They made reports that I was coming, to Louisiana, to take those letters for my children. I was taking my children to say goodbye to their dad. That was it.

People seemed to wonder if I would go to his funeral. Most of them still blamed me for John's crimes. It felt like the victim-blaming would never end.

They said that it was my fault that John was executed because of what he had done. There were those who even said that I shouldn't have gotten a restraining order against him. I should not have divorced him. I should have been the one to help John, as if I could have saved him from himself. In my heart, I knew that only Allah could have helped him. You can't help people who don't want to be helped.

People wanted to know my thoughts and feelings about the whole situation. At the time, I did not want to talk to anyone. Reasonably, I kept to myself.

I had fully healed from the abusive marriage that I had endured with John because I chose to let go of the past. This time was to be spent helping my children cope with knowing their dad was no longer alive. I was there in Louisiana for my children. For me, that is what this was about. We were able to settle into the hotel near the airport.

We made arrangements with one of John's older sons for my children to attend the funeral. We decided that he would come to the hotel to take John, Salena and Taalibah to the funeral. It would be a private ceremony. They kept the location a secret. I had no intentions of going inside the facility. I felt fine with this arrangement. After all, he is my children's half-brother. As long as I knew where my children were and when they'd be back at the hotel, I was fine with them going to the funeral with him.

The next day, he arrived at the hotel. I made sure my children were emotionally, mentally and physically ready to go before releasing them. They seemed to be like me. They were strong. At this point, all they wanted was a chance to say goodbye and a chance to find their peace by having closure.

I felt I made the right decision. I wanted to know where my children would be. I asked John's older son where were the services going to be held.

He said, *"It's a private funeral. I can't tell you because you're not allowed to go to the facility. Dad said, since you had the restraining order against him in life, then we are not allowed to let you in for his death."*

I became angry.

"I have no intentions of going inside," I explained. *"I need to know where my children will be. Even if I bring them to the place, I'll sit in the car. As soon as it's over, we'll leave and be on our way."*

It seemed as if he was becoming angry too. His frustration didn't bother me. I wasn't ready to allow my children to walk away from me without having any information about where they were going. The last time I allowed them to go with someone else, their dad kidnapped them. They were supposed to go for a weekend visit and John did not bring them back to me. Instead, he took them out of the country to Antigua without my permission. I had no knowledge as to where they were and did not see them for 18 months.

My thoughts and reaction may have seemed irrational, but I was afraid. I was not going to allow them to leave without knowing exactly where they would be. I did not trust anyone with them without me. My heart was troubled.

"Please, will you trust me?" John's son pleaded.

"No," I said. *"They are not going with you. I need to know where the funeral is being held. Otherwise, I'll follow you."*

He did not tell me where they were going. I saw the pain in my children's faces. They didn't think I would allow them to go. As I watched them, I looked at his son and said, *"okay, they can go. But I'm following you in my car".* So, we all went outside. My children got into his car and I went to my car. I did as I said I was going to do. I followed them to the funeral. He actually tried to lose me. But, he didn't. I understood why he couldn't tell me where the funeral was being held, to a point. It was a privacy issue, I get that. Still, my children are my first priority. I was angry to have to go through this. But, I had them in my view the whole time.

When we arrived at the facility, I could see the media frenzy had already begun. There was an open lot across the street from the funeral home. People who were attending the funeral were parking there. I decided to park in the last row so no one would see me.

My children were teenagers at the time. There weren't any photographs of them published in the media. Therefore, the media did not bother them and no one recognized them. They were able to walk right past the reporters and the cameras. I felt a great deal of relief as I watched them walk into the funeral home without being harassed by anyone.

As I waited for them, I prayed for Allah to keep them calm and protect their hearts. I could feel God's Spirit move over me. It felt like a calming, peaceful sense of serenity had been draped over me. In that moment, I knew this feeling meant that my children were finding their peace and gaining closure.

I closed my eyes and said, *"Thank you, Allah!"*

The reporters were waiting outside. People began coming out of the funeral facility. That indicated it was over. They were being harassed by the reporters as they tried to stop people to talk to them. They wanted to snap pictures of them and get statements from everyone, but no one complied.

My son, John, called me on the phone. He said that he, Salena and Taalibah were taken out of the back doors of the funeral home so that they could avoid the unwanted attention from the media. He told me to leave now and they would meet me back at the hotel. Quietly, I left the parking lot and drove to the hotel.

They met me at the hotel. I was glad to have them back with me. I opened myself up to their emotions and carefully listened to them. Whatever they wanted to say and express, I was ready to hear them. They expressed their grief in their own way. They cried. They clung to me and accepted the comfort that I had no hesitation to give them. There weren't many words, but lots of emotion and I could feel everything they felt because of my empathy for them. I truly felt for them. They thanked me for bring them to the funeral.

John asked, *"Mom, can we go to the family dinner?"*

I had not considered that there was going to be a repast. At this point, I felt as if I was being tested throughout this whole ordeal. I was on an incredibly emotional ride when it came to wanting to protect them and having to battle with allowing them to continue their healing journey during *their* time of loss.

"Mom, please will you trust us?" He pleaded with me. *"I promise that we will come back."*

"We really want to meet dad's side of the family. We haven't even had a chance to talk to them," Taalibah said.

I really did not know what to say or what to do at that moment. It was true, they hadn't met John's family. I knew that they had the right to get to know their other family.

My children had survived the funeral and came back to me. They seemed fine. I was afraid of how John's family would treat them if I had let them go spend an extended amount of time with them. I had worried because some of them blamed me for John's execution. Again, I asked Allah to help me. Right when I asked, a small voice, from within my spirit, said, *"Let them go!"*

I smiled lovingly at my son, John, and said, *"Okay, you all can go meet your other family. Just be sure to call me to let me know when you're on the way back to the hotel."*

They were grateful for my permission to go to the repast. They hugged me, thanked me, and told me that they would definitely call. And with that, they were gone...

While they were gathering with their dad's relatives, I decided to go to visit my family. I hadn't told them beforehand that I was going to be in town. Therefore, it proved to be a great surprise for them when I showed up at their door.

I visited with my cousin Berthella, my Aunt Rosa Lee, along with Michael and April. Michael and April were my two favorite cousins while growing up. I could not describe how wonderful it was to see all of them again.

Berthella was gladly welcoming. She opened her home to me and invited me to sit down with her. I felt my spirit calming around her. We relaxed in the living room and took some time to reminisce. I told her that I came back to town with my children for John's funeral. She said she understood.

"Well, where are the children?" She asked.

I said, *"They are with John's family at the repast. I let them go. They needed to go."*

"It's good that you let your children spend time with John's family. I know how hard that must've been for you."

She said while nodding her head, *"You did right by them. They are you and John's beautiful children that you created together. God has blessed you with the three of them".*

"Yes, ma'am," I said.

She calmly smiled. Then she shifted her demeanor. Her tone became more serious.

She said, *"Mildred, you know, when you called Michael, and told him your children were taken by John and he had to help you to find them, I was in such pain. I told him to find your babies. I prayed all the time for him to find your children. I know you called him because he's a private investigator."*

"Thank you," I said. *"Thank you for your prayers. We needed everyone's prayers. God certainly did hear them all."*

She said, *I had watched the news and kept up with what had happened. All I could do was pray for you. Mildred, I'm so proud of you."*

"For what?" I asked. I was shocked.

"I'm proud of you for looking after your children. You did what you were taught", she replied.

She seemed to understand me. I didn't have to say much. It felt like it had been a long time since someone took the time to understand me and put themselves in my shoes. I had forgotten what it was like to be shown that kind of empathy and compassion. Berthella stood up and walked over to me. She wrapped her arms around me and squeezed me gently.

I was reminded of how I held my children in my arms when they cried over the past few months. I thought of how I had comforted them and didn't have to ask them how they were feeling because I had already known just by looking at them. Without asking them why, I let them cry.

Now, Berthella was holding me. I felt safe and comforted. I felt like it was okay to open myself up and express my emotions freely. It was the first time in a long time that I let my guards down. I allowed myself to be in that moment with her. I didn't hold back my emotions because I didn't feel the need to do so.

She pulled away from me slightly so that she could look me in the eyes. The calm and warm smile she had before returned to her face.

She said, *"You know, with everything that you're doing, you should know we are proud of you. You're doing great work out there. You help other victims. The services they have now, they didn't exist years ago. You are making a difference! We are your family and we are very proud of you!"*

"Thank you," was all I could say. I was overwhelmed with emotions of joy, love and relief. I was holding back my tears.

"You know who else would be proud?"

I looked up at her and waited for her to tell me.

"Your mother would be very proud of you. I know that she would be proud of all of your hard work as a mother and for the lives of the people that you are saving."

I couldn't hold back anymore; I began to cry. She

pressed the button that released my tears. She continued to hold me as she encouraged me to continue doing my work. She told me not to let anyone stop me. I assured her that my intentions were to continue to work hard, that my work is my purpose.

As ease and comfort began to set in, I stopped crying. We talked about my advocacy work, helping victims of domestic violence and my speaking engagements. I had many plans for me and my children moving forward with the next chapter of our lives. We were on the path of moving through a portal of healing.

I needed that comfort from my family. That was the missing piece. All these years of fighting on my own, the comfort of my family assuring me that everything would be alright, that they were proud of me and that my mother would have been proud of me, were the missing pieces of my healing.

The next day, I brought John, Salena and Taalibah over to visit with my family. It was their first-time meeting Aunt Rosa Lee and cousins Michael, Gwendolyn and April. Berthella wanted to see them before we returned home.

It didn't take long for my children to feel comfortable and right at home with my family. Berthella's kind and welcoming presence helped with that. My girls sang for everyone. We shared memories and funny stories. My children learned more about my family and what life was like for me growing up. It felt wonderful to see my children and my family all gathered together. I hadn't realized how much I missed everyone until we were all together on that day. It was an exceptionally good first meeting for them.

I promised my family that we would try to come visit more often. Perhaps we could visit during the summer while my children were out of school. They seemed pleased and thankful for my offer.

Our visit proved to be a perfect balance of loving support for us. I learned new things about myself during my visit with them. It all made sense why I felt the way I did about my children. Berthella made it clear to me. She confirmed that I was a good mother. I was a good person. I had the courage to let my Spirit guide me. And my children had the privilege of meeting both sides of their families. They were welcomed with open and loving arms. Our visit turned out to be more joyous than I had expected.

We received the comforting solace of togetherness with our families. I was very grateful for that blessing of peace and closure not only for my children, but for myself as well. As the days moved along, there were still other difficulties to overcome.

MILDRED D. MUHAMMAD

CHAPTER 4

OVERCOMING DIFFICULTIES

John's execution and funeral was over. John's hold of terror and pain was behind me. As far as I was concerned, the only way to move was onward and forward. Giving up was **NOT** an option!

As my children would move forward without the presence of their father in their lives, I would move forward without the fear of knowing that John was out there trying to kill me. I did not feel the need to run, hide nor isolate myself. My concentration was focused on my children and our healing.

As I was sitting at the table, I decided to throw away unwanted papers and receipts I kept in my wallet. I saw my restraining order neatly folded in a pocket. The restraining order remained in my wallet even after John was in prison and put on trial. Anyone who has a restraining order should carry the order with them, at all times. Violating a restraining order is *"suppose"* to result in an arrest. I was thinking over the reasons I had it with me. Prior to being captured, he could have shown up at my doorstep. I would call the police stating he had violated my restraining order. Once he was captured, there were reports of failed escape attempts. I know the paper wasn't a bullet proof vest, but it was all I had to convince law enforcement that I needed protection.

Now that John was gone, I decided it was time to throw it away. As soon as I threw it in the trash, it felt like a weight had been lifted from my spirit. The darkness continued to dissolve. My world became a lot brighter and my wallet was lighter too. I considered the action to be another step in my healing.

In January 2010, I ask my second husband, Reuben, for a divorce. Although divorce is a difficult process, the time had come to end the marriage.

I thought that it would have lasted. However, our marriage was a struggle and I was no longer willing to be unhappy. I saw the marriage as a learning experience. The divorce settled in January 2012.

Divorce is a life altering decision. Life goes on and the rebuilding of my life and of my children's lives continued. In making that change, I began to understand more about myself and what I want in a relationship.

I decided that I was going to enjoy my time alone. I was in a much better place than where I had been before. I was struggling in a marriage that wasn't going anywhere. Gaining this understanding and having peace of mind gave me the courage to keep going. I felt empowered! I learned that I was the one who will decide who rents space in mind. I am the one who decides how I choose to react to any situation, whether good or bad. And I decided to enjoy my life and accept circumstances as they happen even though I have no control over how others react. Most importantly, I thank God for the gift of learning to love myself. Self-love is key for our survival in this world.

I continued to concentrate on the welfare of my children and build on my relationships with them. They are the most important people in my life. I also dived into my work as an advocate for victims and survivors of domestic violence.

Prior to John's execution, my first speaking engagement was at a Survivor's Forum at Prince George's Community College, on October 26, 2006. Norma Harley had extended a personal invitation to me. Norma emailed me about the event. She was the first victim's advocate in the county years ago. She was putting together the program for Domestic Violence Awareness Month.

I knew about her work. She and I had spoken a few times throughout the year about issues and topics related to domestic violence.

She said, *"I have two speakers presenting at the forum. I need one more speaker to complete the theme for our Domestic Violence Forum on religion. Mildred, I want you to come to the forum and tell your story."*

My response was, *"Are you crazy?"*

I told her, *"People in this community blame me for what happened. I have received so much disrespect and horrible things are being said about me and my children. If I go there, I won't have anyone to protect me."*

She didn't seem fazed, but she listened to my concerns. *"Oh Mildred,"* she said, *"I'll protect you!"*

It was funny to hear her say that because she was shorter than me! I'm only 5 feet and four inches tall! Norma was a tiny woman, but she was bold, brave and serious about what needed to be done. I admired her for her work and I was touched by her belief in me. I agreed to speak at the forum.

With my children there to support me on the front row, I overcame my fear to speak. My children made me feel safe. The response to my contribution to the forum was tremendously positive. To my surprise, it left me feeling refreshed and energized to speak in an open forum about the abuse we suffered. That is when I officially found my voice.

I began speaking at conferences. It was during those times that I had been encouraged by domestic violence organizations and individuals to write a book so that others would be able to benefit from my survivor's story. Perhaps they would read my story and try to avoid the pitfalls I had gone through while running for my life.

With the encouragement I received, I wanted to be excited about my book. It was not just to help others, but it was part of the healing process for me as well. However, it was very painful to go back to that time and think about all that had happened. I didn't want to remember. Therefore, there were times when I didn't want to write.

I decided on the title, *"Scared Silent: When the one you love becomes the one you fear"*. The writing process was slow and painful. Remembering what had happened was not something that I wanted to do every single day. I journaled every day when I lived in the shelter in Tacoma and when I moved to Maryland. To build my story, I selected several pages from my journals to include in my book. I read through my journals and decided what information to share. And I remember how afraid I was to share with the world, my pain, fears and emotions. People would actually read my life story. It wasn't an easy realization to process. I had already experienced rejection, humiliation and victim-blaming. The more I included, the more I felt weary.

My deepest fear, about publishing my story, was the harsh criticism of those who didn't see me and my children as victims because we didn't have physical scars nor were we killed. I decided that I wasn't going to debate with anyone because I truly felt that everyone is entitled to their own opinions and emotions. *Who am I to say how a person should or should not feel?*

Since people were unable to talk to John and ask him for his side of the story, I didn't think I would be putting myself out there as a target with this book. They would be unable to send John a message regarding the hurt, shame and pain they were feeling because he took the lives of innocent people and terrorized a community, the world, my children. I didn't understand that I could be their target once I put my story out there. I didn't know that I had to protect my children from being targeted. I didn't know if I could take it, but I would have to so my children would not be preyed upon.

I kept my faith in Allah and asked Him to guide and strengthen me during the writing process. I asked Him to bless my mind, heart and spirit with peace. I heard the voices of other women in my sleep. I heard the many cries of women who didn't have the physical scars to prove that they were victims.

Many nights, I couldn't sleep because hearing the voices of these women brought back hurtful memories, triggers, and flashbacks from the past. Instead of giving up, I let Allah move my spirit to write out what I was feeling.

Before I knew it, it was done. Just like that, my book was completely written. It felt good to accomplish writing my book. The purpose of writing *Scared Silent* was to assist other victims and survivors in getting out of their abusive situations while recognizing the pitfalls I'd been through so they could avoid them, but the release of my book made me nervous.

My life took a big turn when my first book was scheduled to be released. The decision to release it was made in June 2008. The release date had been set for October 2009. Many people are not aware that October is Domestic Violence Awareness Month and the crimes were committed during the month of October.

The decision was made to release the book in October because *Scared Silent* is about the domestic abuse, child custody and the pain we suffered prior to John coming to the DC metro area. It was not to capitalize from John's execution, as others had accused me of doing.

In business, professionals say that timing is *everything*. We did not anticipate the news of John's execution date and sentence to be released at the same time *Scared Silent* was to be released.

In response, I received verbal insults and disrespectful actions directed towards me and my children when the book was released. It seemed that many people forgot or didn't know about the abuses we had suffered. Once again, the victim-blaming began, but this time it was because I spoke out and told the side of the story the media did not report.

I was no longer *"Scared Silent"*. Therefore, I decided despite what other people were saying, I am going to continue to talk about domestic violence, promote awareness and use our survival story to help people who are victims.

Scared Silent wasn't advertised as much as I had been told. I didn't feel the embrace from people after my book's release. It felt as if the atmosphere was not welcoming for my story. I don't know what I was expecting. Perhaps, I expected too much!

If my book was going to successfully help other victims and survivors of domestic violence, I had to get out and represent it myself. I had to embrace that my book was an open door to my life and the possibility of rejection and judgment was very high. This was an incredibly challenging process for me.

Speaking engagements were already booked for the month of October. The events I attended were welcoming and I was able to tell my story and talk about my book. Even though I smiled on the outside, I cried on the inside.

Whatever my expectations were, I could not forget that it was for the women whose voices called out to me during those sleepless nights. I couldn't focus on what the masses were saying. I had to focus on what those individuals who needed to read my book were saying.

They said that my book helped them. I began to focus, not on what I thought I had expected from others, but the fact that I accomplished the goal behind writing my book. Although I still felt bittersweet, I did start to feel good about helping others with my story.

As I thought of women and the organizations who asked me to write my book, I accepted my story would help many women. Especially those who did not have physical scars as I did. Physical abuse and murder are the end results of domestic violence. It begins with a verbal assault. Eighty percent of victims don't have physical scars. Unfortunately, these are amongst the silent victims who never believe they are victims or report their abuse.

We need to understand that whether it's physical abuse, verbal abuse, psychological abuse, economic abuse, spiritual abuse, mental abuse, sexual abuse, elder abuse, human trafficking, child abuse or stalking, it is all abuse and it must end. *Abuse is abuse!*

My voice became stronger as I continued speaking at domestic violence conferences, workshops, and seminars. My speaking engagements increased and included documentaries and talk shows. This helped me to reach more people who needed help. My emails increased and I always responded within 24 hours. I didn't want anyone to feel like I was leaving them out in the cold as I once felt waiting for a return call. Even today, it's hard for me to turn anyone away when they are in need of help. I try to provide as many resources as I can for those in need.

Unfortunately, many of the organizations that I was connected with had to close their doors. The closings were due to budget cuts, lack of federal grants and donations from the public. Many social programs had to be put on hold or cut because of issues with funding.

Domestic violence has been stigmatized. As a result, these important organizations lack support that they need to stay alive. Many believe that domestic violence issues are private matters and that it should stay within the family, kept within the home.

I remember growing up, it was said, *"What happens at home, stays at home"?* I've heard this many times throughout my life. I've heard many abuse victims say that this was a motto in their home. It is wrong!

It must be understood that regardless of your education or financial status, occupation, race, creed or religion, people in all walks of life are affected by this social dis-ease, yet there seems to be no resolution in sight. We seem to find ourselves constantly reacting instead of *acting* when a case of abuse is reported and it makes national news. Think about the number of unreported abuses.

Unfortunately, it is being made to appear that domestic violence is a poverty issue. The stats on victims and abusers, making income of $250k and above, are difficult to find because the theory is people making income in that bracket and above are not abusers or victims, which it so far from the truth. Victims in this financial status have limited places to go and find themselves isolated from resources designed to assist them as well.

The media concentrates on the life of the abuser, especially if he or she is well-known, in a position of power or a celebrity. They are constantly reporting how successful they are and the struggle they went through to be in their present position. It amazes me, every time, that the victim isn't treated the same way. What are their accomplishments? What did they do to deserve to be killed? And yet, we don't hear anything. But I've noticed, the victim is silenced and is made to feel the need to apologize for what they did. They don't understand that the fault is not theirs. Inaccurate information is reported as well. It's about who gets to report it first. It's about the ratings and sensationalism.

Once the details of the story are presented, then they have to find someone to blame. Usually, the victims are to blame. Once the blame is placed, then the issue of the abuse is discussed. After the sensationalism has simmered down, the story fades away with the abuser attending anger management classes and/or a restraining order without any real solution to or hope for the prevention of domestic violence and abuse. There isn't a report on the status or what is being done to help the victim. We don't hear it...at all!

Some believe women have a choice and chose to be abused. There are more shelters for animals than there are for victims of domestic violence. And then question becomes, why should victims have shelters? The theory is that animals don't have a choice and are unable to move away from the abuse because of their loyalty to their owner. However, women don't have a choice when finances and children are involved. And most times, the psychological abuse and fear can be so detrimental, it paralyzes them from leaving. Up to 75% of abused women are murdered after they leave their partners.

It's a very disturbing cycle that continues to repeat itself each time a serious incident occurs. We must get serious about this issue. Women and children are dying every day.

The question that remains is: *How can we prevent abuse before it is taken to the level of mutilating or killing someone?* No one knows who will be the next abuser to cross the line from verbally assaulting to maiming or killing someone.

Preventing domestic violence and abuse should begin in the home and in school. It must begin in elementary school, as we teach our children about healthy relationships. All relationships should be discussed including friendships, relationships with relatives, immediate family, teachers and authority figures, etc. Breaking the cycle of abuse is crucial!

Our children will carry the torch for our future. We want our children to be better than what this world has told them they should become. We want them to make the world a much better place to live in with their love, presence and contribution. Most of all, we want our children to treat themselves and others better, starting with respect. And having faith in the process is a good place to start.

MILDRED D. MUHAMMAD

CHAPTER 5

HAVING FAITH IN THE PROCESS

"Faith is being sure of the things we hope for and knowing that something is real even if we don't see it." Hebrews 11:1

I'm reminded of the story of the soldier coming to Jesus to heal his daughter because she was sick. Jesus' reply to the soldier was, *"Because of your faith, your daughter is healed."*

The soldier's daughter was miles away from him, Jesus and his disciples. Even though it took him days to get back to his daughter, the soldier still believed. When he returned home, his daughter was in fact healed. He had great faith.

That is the kind of faith that I've worked hard to achieve. I study the Holy Quran and the Holy Bible. Today, this is the kind of faith that I carry with me. It did not happen for me overnight. It took time, strength and courage to build.

Circumstances arise to test our faith. Making the decision to trust and believe that everything will work out in your favor, is stepping out on faith. Each time I step out on faith, I know that in time, my prayers will be answered. Every day, my faith continues to grow.

The Qur'an says that Allah will add faith to your faith. I know, with full assurance, that Allah will answer my prayers every day. When my prayers are answered, my faith increases. When I'm praying for a door to open, if the door doesn't open, I know it's not my door. When issues arise, I know I will be alright. My faith carries me through the experience. I don't question any situation anymore. Scripture assures me, as it says, *"You have not because you ask not."* I ask and receive without a doubt.

Complete healing was in store for me. With faith, healing was a reality for myself and my children.

What did it take? I had to go deep inside. I went into the essence of my spirit. I uprooted the pain that had such a strong grip on my life. This pain caused me to have a distorted view of the world. Pain is what kept me in *the isolation,* that dark and lonely place.

I was afraid to open myself to anyone because there was no one whom I felt comfortable or safe to talk to at that point. Pain and fear made me feel as if I'd be judged, rejected and made to feel like the things that had happened were my fault. I didn't want to be blamed and made to feel ashamed for those terribly, tragic events.

To process through this, I had two plans. The first plan was to allow myself to heal from the emotional trauma that I experienced. The second was to help my children in their healing. Honestly, I knew that I was a mess inside. And since I was a mess, my children were too. My healing was important for my success and the success of my children. They are my motivators. They always have been and they always will be the wind beneath my wings. They give me flight.

When I look back on when they were missing, I went to people who I called *"friends"* for help. They told me that John told them I would be coming to them for help and to ignore me. He told them that he took our children because I wasn't taking care of them and they would be better off with him. Their responses to me were, *"Why are you saying these bad things about John? At least you can just cook for one. Snap out of it and go back to work. You're young, you can have more children".*

This was hurtful and disappointing. Hearing these

comments discouraged me and it was a setback in my healing. *How could I begin to heal when I didn't know where my children were? And how could they say such terrible things to me? What did I do to deserve that kind of treatment?*

Only those who understand the numerous emotions, that consume your mind and body, when you find out your child or children have been taken away, can understand my pain. Those who have to lay their heads to a pillow every night, not knowing where their children are. Those who know the pain of closing their eyes to sleep and feeling guilty. Those who are only existing and not living, waiting to hear the voices of their children again, to grasp the touch of their hands, to see the smile on their faces, truly understand how I felt. Yet, I had to find a way to stay strong and healthy as I waited for the return of my children.

How could they tell me to snap out it? How would they react had their children been taken? How could a mother look me in my face and tell me that?

I isolated myself from everyone. I felt so alone. I did not lose my faith. God was all I had. I continued to pray asking for people and resources to be put in place to help me.

There was this new thing called *"the internet"*. I decided to give it a try and look up information that would help me. I found an interesting site and joined an online forum on www.blackvoices.com. I watched the conversations for a while. When I felt comfortable, I began telling people, whom I didn't know, what was happening. Behold, there were lawyers, advocates and others who either knew someone who was experiencing the same thing or just giving advice. They offered words of encouragement and told me everything would be alright. They were glad to see me when I entered the room and began asking how I was feeling and telling me the next steps to take. They were my angels. They helped me get through my day. My prayer had been answered. My healing began because I had people to talk to and they didn't judge me or make me feel that the abuse or that the fact that my children were taken, was my fault. Sometimes strangers can be more of a friend or family than your own.

I was trying to figure out things on my own and little by little, it was coming together. I had a lot to learn and I had to learn it quickly. Healing was coming at my pace.

There were some who came to me and insisted that I take John back making ridiculous claims that he loves me. I said to them, since you love him so much, you can have him. I was not taking him back. Had I listened to them, I would not be alive today. I'm so glad I listened to my spirit and took a stand.

He talked a good game and convinced them that I was the problem. The sad part is that they believed him! They took his side and felt he was justified in his actions. They even assisted him in taking my children by giving him money and lying to me about it. They hid him, with our children, at their homes and said, to my face, *"if they knew where John and my children were, they would tell me"*. They knew and didn't tell me.

I began to trust my own instinct and decided to do things the way I thought they should be done. I didn't listen to anyone who didn't see it my way. It didn't matter to me who they were. If you were not supporting me, then you are supporting John and you do not belong in my life. I had a right to be angry, I had a right to cry, I had a right to know where my children were. Anyone who tried to stop me from moving in a manner that I decided to go, I no longer communicated with them. That's how I had to move forward and it would prove to be the best way for me. That was my process.

I relied on Allah for strength. I encouraged myself to maintain my emotions to obtain the kind of healing that I saw forthcoming. No one would understand, without judging and associating me with John, *"The D.C. Sniper"*.

I needed so much to be heard. Allah heard my cries. In the Qur'an there is the story of Jacob. Jacob had 12 sons, one of them was named Joseph. One day, Joseph went missing, although his other sons knew where he was, they didn't tell him. Jacob put his faith in God saying, *"I complain only to Allah."*

When I read that, my spirit began to calm. That passage had to have been for me to read at that moment. I knew what it was like to be in that kind of pain. The pain of losing your children. I was encouraged by Jacob's words. Allah is the only one who could answer my prayers, encourage me and heal my spirit.

Everyone has their own process when circumstances arise that need their attention. I'm often asked, after a presentation, how I handled my situation well enough to actually get through it. I will share my steps to ensure my healing. However, keep in mind, everyone has a process that works best for themselves. My way of processing faith and healing may not work for you because we are all made in our own unique way. We process information differently. That's part of the beauty of life that God has given us.

It is important for all of us, who are going through the healing process to understand, accept and embrace that we heal in different ways and at our own pace. Don't allow anyone to establish a timeline for your healing. Also, don't let anyone, not even yourself, minimize your situation nor your pain. You have a right to your emotions, how you grieve and process your faith to healing. And most of all, don't compare your situation or your pain to anyone else.

My process of self-healing and self-encouragement began by releasing all betrayals, bitterness and resentful emotions that I had towards myself and others. First, I had to learn different ways of coping to encourage myself. If I waited for someone else to save me, I would still be waiting. So, I had to find an outlet for myself. I found my outlets through music, dancing, laughter, praying and journaling.

While I remain a huge advocate for journaling, I must admit, when I listen to music, it helps me release emotions in a way that journaling does not. I mostly listened to smooth jazz. I noticed, at that time, listening to music with words, had a negative effect on my healing. When I listened to old-school R&B and love songs, I realized that they could set off triggers. So, I stopped listening to music with words. It was better for me, at that time for my healing.

I remember listening to a smooth jazz radio channel while in the shelter. I was journaling about how much I missed my children and how being in the shelter was affecting me. I was writing out a plan on what actions I needed to take to get my children back. Suddenly, a gospel song began playing on the *"smooth jazz channel"*. The cords in the music captivated my spirit. I wasn't sure who it was.

The words were, *'I remember the first time, you laughed with me. I remember the promises you would never leave my side. Now I'm standing with the news of a tragedy, standing here with a fragile heart."*

When I heard those words, I realized my heart was broken. I couldn't put a name to the pain I was feeling until that moment. I stopped writing and began crying uncontrollably. It would take two weeks before I heard it again and finally found out the artist. The song is called *"Fragile Heart"* by Yolanda Adams. That song became one of the tools I used to dive deep into my faith.

The chorus of the song continues,
"When I think about, think about life, Lord I think of you I forget about everything else, there's only you and I And I can't think about ever giving up, Can't give up the fight (no, no). The only thing that matters Lord, is YOU"!

I began to release my children and my whole situation into Allah's hands. Every time I listened to this song, it became a different level of release for me.

We were not allowed to have music playing when we left our rooms. I asked permission for this song to play, continuously, as it was a huge part of my healing. The staff understood and granted the permission. I didn't have a roommate, so that made it even better. After a while, I memorized the words so now they are ingrained in my heart. I didn't find out until much later that this song was a tribute to Ms. Yolanda Adams' mother's transitioning. I looked at it as a way to handle the absence of my children while releasing them to Allah to take care of them for me. Now that I'm healed, I can listen to all genres of music without it affecting me in any negative way. I no longer have those triggers. I even find joy in dancing to some of those songs.

Dancing is the universal language of the world. It's a way of expression and identity. It is certainly one of my passions. I love to dance as it played a big role in my healing process.

When I hear music and I like the beat, I move some part of my body. Even when I was a little girl, I used music as a fun motivator to clean up and practice new dance moves.

When I was living in the shelter, it was time to clean. We had a chore list. Each person's name was next to the area that they were responsible for. When I completed my part, I went to my room to clean. I've always cleaned to music, so I can dance and clean at the same time. For me, it made cleaning more fun to do. One of the ladies was playing the *"Thriller"* album by Michael Jackson. My favorite song, on the CD came on which is, to this day, *"PYT (Pretty Young Thing)"*. I stopped cleaning and just started doing all the dances I knew. Moonwalk, pop locking, bus stop, etc. They decided to play it continuously because they saw my reaction to it. I danced, nonstop for two hours! I don't know what came over me. I danced the same, fast pace, for that amount of time. I felt such an emotional release. I was dancing my pain away.

Even as I'm writing, I'm smiling because I remember the emotions going through my body. All the pain being released regarding my children, the fear of knowing John was going to kill me and the fact that I was living in a shelter for protection. It all came out as I was dancing. Once I stopped dancing, I was exhausted. I took a long shower and slept the rest of the day. I didn't awaken until the morning. I felt refreshed, refocused and prepared for the day. I love to dance. It is my source of release!

I remember when I was blessed to get my children back. We were listening to music in the living room. PYT came on and I got up to dance. My children had not seen me dance in a long time. They watched for a while, then they got up to dance with me. It was the icebreaker I needed to get them to open up. Just then, my son began to moon walk. I stopped dancing and watched him with the biggest smile. I asked him where did he learn that? He shrugged his shoulders, laughed and continued to dance. My girls were amazing at how well I was dancing. I reminded them that I won a dance contest or two in my day. We all laughed. That was the best day because they opened up and allowed me back into their hearts. It was an amazing day that I will always treasure.

When my children were missing, I was so sad. Depression was knocking on my door. I missed them so, so much. At times, I wondered if I was still a mother. I didn't watch the serious tv shows I was accustomed to watching. They were filled with triggers. I felt I needed to laugh.

I watched, 'The Kings of Comedy". The comedians were Steve Harvey, Cedric The Entertainer, Bernie Mac and D. L. Hughley. That was the funniest show I had seen. I laughed so hard, I fell off the sofa.

The Tom Joyner Show helped me during the trial. They made jokes about everything. J Anthony Brown was hilarious. After my book was released, I was interviewed on their show and was awarded, "Thursday Morning Mom" for protecting my children. The $1,000 prize helped to buy new clothes, shoes and school supplies for my children and put food in our home. I was truly struggling. That award helped us so much.

I continued to watch funny shows. "Friends" became

the show I would watch the most. Every time I watched, something they did or said, caused me to laugh. That is one funny show.

Journaling was major in my growth and development in the healing process. Journaling is my therapy. The journal doesn't talk back, doesn't judge me and it's a safe place to deposit all my emotions. Getting to the root of my pain was my objective. For me, my pain was like an onion. The core, of that onion, is the root of my pain. Pulling back each layer exposed the depth of my pain. The closer I was getting to the core, the harder my journey became. However, if I wanted to heal, I had to go through, not over, not around, nor under the pain and it was very traumatically long process.

My desire was to be completely healed from all the abuse I suffered. My abuse was not physical. Many don't understand that eighty percent of victims don't have physical scars. An emotional hit can last throughout your life. I've seen how it prevents others from moving forward. Symptoms such as flashbacks, nightmares, living in a heightened state of fear and being unable to break free are some of the results of the trauma. That's not what I wanted for my life. That's not what I wanted for my children's lives. Triggers are everywhere. Recognizing your triggers and how they affect you will change the dynamics of your healing.

I was determined to live emotionally balanced. I was not going to carry bags around with John's name on them. I was determined not to judge every man by the actions that I experienced with John. That would not be fair. I wanted to be able to look at each person, without a pre-conceived notion of what they would or would not do, but to view them as they presented themselves. My reactions would only be based upon what they say or do. They would be the only ones who would change my perspective of who they are.

My courage and strength came because of journaling. I found journaling to be the most effective tool I use to heal. Because we are a visual people, meaning if I can't see my pain, then my pain does not exist, putting my thoughts on paper, gave me the opportunity to see just how much pain I was in. Having an avenue to express how I felt, uninterrupted, was my saving grace. By diving deeply into my pain, my trauma, I was able to uproot such emotions as guilt, shame, and unworthiness as well as the victim-blaming and hurtful comments me and my children were exposed to by so many others.

Emotions such as shame, guilt, anger, fear and other negative emotions, have a different meaning after trauma. These are the kind of emotions that made me dislike myself. They also robbed me of my confidence. Negative emotions are natural, just like positive ones. It was important for me to get a clear understanding of the emotion I was feeling so I could heal from it. I didn't want to continue to cry over the same situation. I wasn't being fair to myself or my growth.

Although these words have many definitions, I read each one until the meaning resonated with my spirit. That's when I knew I found the right one. I studied the meaning until I had a firm grip on my emotions. I applied the understanding of that emotion to my situation then questioned myself as to why did I feel that way. I found I was taking on emotions that weren't mine to keep. So, once I understood that, I was able to let them go, out of my system…never to feel them again. I released them to Allah. I took my burdens to the Lord and left them there. My faith was the one bright spot in my life. The Qur'an says that Allah is as close to you as your jugular vein. I am never alone.

An excerpt, from my journal:

"*I've been praying to Allah to lift this spirit of depression that has come over me. I submitted my fears and anxieties to Him and I feel better. I know He will comfort me. I know, as the day progresses, He will answer me. There is no one I trust, love and adore more than Allah. I'm grateful for His love for me. Everything that has taken away from me, I found out, I can survive. I also found out that Allah was with me the entire time and at times sent angels to comfort me, both physically and spiritually. I know this is a process that I am experiencing and Allah will see me through it. I'm truly grateful. I love you Allah and thank you for loving me. And please don't turn away from me for surely, I would be of the losers. This is my praise of thanksgiving. Salaam (Peace)"*

As I was writing, more emotions were coming up that I didn't even realize were there. Negative emotions such as hate, anxious, confusion, misery, and others were coming to the forefront of my mine and were taking a toll on me. I didn't stop writing at that point. I needed relief. As I continued to write, more understanding came because of those additional emotions. This was going to be a long journey I decided to embark upon, the healing of myself.

Understanding, accepting and embracing my *"whole self"*, which included my strengths and weaknesses would help with my heart and spirit being repaired because both were broken! My confidence began to grow as well as the love I have for myself. As time moved on, I learned to replace the negative emotions with positive ones *(joy, love, peace, happiness)*. I would find out, much later, that I was better prepared for the overwhelming emotions to come when I got my children back.

Through journaling, I was able to move strategically through my emotions, experiencing them head on and understanding how they affected myself and the lives of my children. Journaling kept me encouraged.

Encouragement is to give support and hope to yourself and others. I wanted to help other people. However, I had to find the courage and strength within myself before I could pass along wisdom and encouragement to anyone else.

History had shown me that those who knew my circumstances, didn't value me as a person. And at that time, I didn't know how to value myself. I know that going into despair is a sin. I didn't lose hope even though I didn't know where my children were. I was fighting for my life, my sanity.

If I allowed my depression to consume me and I would continue to spiral downward into a mental pit I could not come out of. I would not be able to raise my children. I could not keep going down the same road, falling in the same hole and expect a different reality. That is surely insanity.

I began to learn how to trust myself. Trust in my ability to make things happen. I used the internet to look up information about my situation and applied it. It worked. The more I practiced handling my situation myself, the more my confidence grew as well as my self-esteem.

When I did seek out help and they told me they could not help me, I found another way. No one will have the passion to find out what I need to do for me and my children or care about me or my situation more than I would. I was scared. I decided to used my fear as fuel that would drive me to uncover solutions to my problems that others said they could not do. So, the word **'NO'** became my fuel to dig deeper and come out with a better way to solve my problems.

In order to continue to free my spirit from negative emotions and allow positivity into my life, I had to learn to let go. My objective was to allow the freeing of my emotions and spirit through creativity and spirituality.

One of the benefits of spirituality is gaining understanding of myself. It is understanding how, where and why I exist and feeling every emotion that comes. My Spirit helped me to understand how much I've changed and everything that I've experienced. It took a lot of time for me to gain understanding, and realize what I needed to do for us. Also, it allowed me to strengthen my relationship with Allah. Praying, fasting, writing, speaking and helping others are major steps in my process of continued growth and healing.

Praying is my personal conversation with Allah. I tell Him everything. I thank Him for everything. I share my joy and my pain with Him. When I make my prayers, I feel much better afterwards. When I'm troubled, I say this short prayer throughout the day, *"My prayer, my sacrifice, my life and my death are all for Allah, the Lord of the Worlds. No associate has He and this I am commanded and I am of those who submit."* And right after the last word, I feel comforted, at peace and convinced that Allah is fighting my battles for me. Whenever I'm troubled, going to Him in prayer has become the best solution. I trust and believe that Allah knows what He is doing with my life. I accept and move forward knowing that when I release my faith, I know with assurance, that *ALL* circumstances will work in my favor every day.

Just because the issue doesn't look like it is in my favor, in the physical, doesn't mean that it's not working spiritually. I don't know nor am I able to see the big picture. That's what having faith in the process means. I know in time; I will understand it better by and by. I believe that I'm guided. Allah knows exactly what the solutions are. Again, I have no choice other than to trust Him. I have faith in the process.

Fasting is the purification of my mind, body and spirit. My children call me a professional faster since I fast often. The longest fast I've completed is 30 days. The shortest is three days.

In every religion, we are told to fast and pray. I believe that food can be a blockage from hearing God clearly. We can get in the habit of concentrating on food more than connecting to God. Fasting has become my way of connecting to Allah on a spiritual level. I've noticed that when I fast, my body is lighter, my mind is clearer, I'm more aware and grateful for the blessings and favor. Toxins are being removed from my body when I fast. I know some doctors don't recommend fasting but why would Allah say it's okay?

Again, this is my faith guiding me. I'm doing what's best for me. Everyone may not agree with how or what I do. That's okay. This is part of my process. Making the decision to take care of myself the way I feel is best for me takes discipline and a strong will to continue even when others don't agree.

Everyone's entitled to their own way of healing and their own opinions. We make our own choices. We don't always have to agree. I used to be a people-pleaser, but not anymore. At this point in my life, I only seek to please Allah. And in pleasing Him, I know that everything else is taken care of. *"Seek ye 'first' the kingdom of God and ALL of His righteousness and everything shall be given unto you"*. This is where I am!

Allah supplies all of my needs and he has blessed me with many gifts. In having faith and getting through the process, I have used my gifts to help others.

I've learned to rely on God instead of relying upon others and my own understanding. I relied on God and He gave me the strength and knowledge to be wise to move forward. I am able to be alone since Allah gave me the opportunity to self-reflect, meditate, accept my life and grow from the mistakes I've made in my past. I am strong because of the trails Allah has seen me through.

The most rewarding gifts that I have received from Him are insight, my beautiful children, love and my relationship with Him.

Allah has blessed me to make it through with His grace and mercy. Allah is the true source of my strength. This is the constant truth of my life. Allah's love remains consistent and never waivers or fails.

He didn't bring me this far to abandon me as I felt so many others had left me and my family. The truth is, people come into our lives for a reason, a season and a lifetime. Some relationships, whatever they may be, may only be for a moment and some may last for a lifetime. Once the reason and the season is up, you'll notice they are no longer around. Their purpose, in your life, is complete. I understand and accept this truth.

From the relationships that I had and still do maintain, I take with me the lessons I've learned from the past. These lessons are part of my gifts that Allah has blessed me with.

Living, maturing and learning from relationships and our life experiences is part of earning the gift of wisdom.

During this process, I did not want to squander the precious time that God gave to me. Therefore, I had to put myself on a schedule that would encompass my daily life. Time management is one of the key components of the process. I used my time wisely by continuing to write, reflect, meditate, spend time with my family, worship and help others.

In the beginning, speaking was a difficult and scary process for me especially because of the many negative comments I had received. Victim-blaming was very high for me. When I look back at all the conferences, trainings, workshops and seminars I've participated in, I can say that Norma Harley gave me my start. I will be forever grateful to her kind spirit and big heart. She only had kind words of encouragement for me. I miss her dearly and so does her family.

Norma passed in 2012. Her family asked me to say a few words at her memorial. I was grateful for the opportunity to share with her loved ones what she did for me. Thanks to Norma, speaking plays another major part in this process that has assisted me in completely healing from *everything* I went through.

Now, I share my expertise on what it's like to be a victim and a survivor of domestic violence *"without physical scars"* to various conferences, seminars, workshop audiences which include victims and survivors of domestic violence, advocates, law enforcement professionals, therapists, counselors, mental and medical health providers, university and college students as well as conduct military personnel training regarding domestic violence. I explain the perils of PTSD (*post-traumatic stress disorder*) soldiers suffer when returning from a war zone as well as victims who are diagnosed with PTSD. I am at a point in my life where I can share my story of triumph and walk away without any residue such as nightmares, flashbacks, and emotional pain. To get to this place in my process, it required a lot of personal development.

Many people feel that when you are a victim of domestic abuse or violence, you are not good decision-makers. A part of taking my life back included me owning my opinions, feelings, thoughts, decision-making and the way I decide to process them all. My experience had been others deciding to express their opinions in a way that would blame or criticize me as well as questioning my ability to take care of myself and my children. I realized and still do that people are entitled to their opinions. That doesn't mean that I have to accept, internalize or put into practice what is said. I've taught this principle to my children as well.

I've heard comments along the lines of, *"If he hits you once, you don't leave, but if he hits you again, then you are a volunteer."* That is cruel! *How can someone blame the victim for the abuse?* I had to learn, on my own, that I did not have to accept advice from others if I didn't want to. That's my right and my decision. They didn't live with me nor did they know the abuse I was suffering. The most important issue for a victim is having someone to believe them.

Some people can be very judgmental. They judge from the limited experience they have had in their lives. Therefore, if they haven't experienced any type of abuse, they are quick to make statements to indicate that it is the victims' fault. I listen to what is being said. If there is something I can use in my personal development, I'll keep what is needed and allow the rest to fall away.

I have learned that it is easier for bystanders to blame the victim and difficult to confront the abuser. The victim is already beaten down, physically and emotionally. They see what the abuser has done to the victim and they want no part of that. *Why not confront the abuser?*

There are very few cases where the family of the victim came to her rescue. Many victims experience their friends and families turning their backs on them. Some of them take the side of the abuser even after knowing everything that has been done to the victim. They invite the abuser to family functions, knowing the victim will be there. They will be upset that the victim is upset because the abuser was invited. Some would say, *just because he/she hurt you doesn't mean we can't like him/her.* Crazy…I know!

One of my favorite quotes is, *"To thine own self be true."* I decided that I have to be true to myself before I can be true to anyone else. To me, it means that I have to trust my own instincts, my own opinions, even if no one else does. I must understand who I am and where I'm going, even if no one else agrees. No one persons' opinion, regarding my life, is more important than my own. I learned to be patient and trust myself. It is fine if no one agrees with my way of doing what I felt I needed to do for me and my children.

During my time at the shelter, I was diagnosed with Post Traumatic Stress Disorder (PTSD). PTSD is a term I'd only heard once and that is when John was diagnosed with it when he returned from Desert Storm. Now, I had it. I had to educate myself and learn about what it means for me. I began my research to learn what I could do to help myself.

A disorder meant it was something within my mind that was out of order and needed correction. I knew the event that took place, put me in this position. I decided to learn more about PTSD and then learn how to overcome it.

According to the Anxiety & Depression Association of America website, *(www.adaa.org)*, *"PTSD is a serious potentially debilitating condition that occur in people who have experienced or witnessed a natural disaster, serious accident, terrorist incident, sudden death of a loved one, war; or rape or other violent personal assault"*. Which means it's not unusual to have flashbacks, nightmares or intrusive memories.

I continued my research through the internet. There wasn't as much information on PTSD when John was diagnosed in 1992. Research, medication and therapy had come a long way in 2000. While medication may help other people, I decided that medication is not for me.

I was glad to know that I was not alone in this diagnosis and read how there was some success in overcoming it. Some PTSD is so severe for many people, that living day to day is a feat within itself, as I was for two years. That explained my condition. I was hunted like an animal for two years, not sure if I would live or die before finding my children. I was always in a heightened sense of fear. That time was the scariest period in my life. I will never be that afraid again. I was totally terrified of John. No one could calm me because I knew who I was dealing with. But because John only showed me that side of him, the side he showed others caused them to believe him and question me. Only three people, out of all the friends we had, believe me.

According to ADAA, some symptoms are: *flashbacks, night sweats, nightmares, intrusive memories. Also, negative beliefs, guilt and self-blame, and a persistent negative emotional state. Feeling emotionally numb and avoiding situations or activities that are reminders of the trauma, loss of interest in everything, withdrawing from family or friends for months or years.* I had these symptoms.

Some people decide that suicide is better than living with these symptoms. They fight every day to live. I remember sharing my story at a military installation because there's a military component involved. Twenty-two soldiers commit suicide a day. That's a number we don't like to discuss and not reported enough. I share this statistic in my presentation, at military installations, as well as encouraging others to get help if they need it.

I remember speaking at a military installation, a few years ago. When my presentation was over, I shook hands and posed for pictures with some of the personnel who attended the presentation. Some of them were moved to share their personal stories with me and ask questions. One soldier shook my hand and thanked me for sharing my story.

He said, *"your words touched me so, so much"*. Then he leaned over closer to me and said, *"Ms. Muhammad, my life isn't worth living and I'm at ground zero. When I leave here, I'm going to kill myself"*, then tried to walk away."

I held onto his hand and said, *"No Sir, not today! Will you please allow me to talk to your Commander about you? See, he's right over there. Will you allow me to do that while you have a seat? I won't be long!"*

He said, *"Yes ma'am."*

I went to the Commander and explained to him what the soldier whispered to me. There were counselors at the presentation. He responded to him immediately. They were able to help him right then and there. That was encouraging to watch and see that there was help available for him ready and in place when he needed it. From what I have heard from my contacts, the soldier responded favorably to the help that he was given and he is now doing well.

If you are feeling alone, like no one cares and you have no one to talk to; don't allow suicide to be your form of escape. Seek out help. There is always someone available to talk to you.

The National Suicide Prevention Lifeline number is 800-273-8255. Since we all live through our smart-phones, there's an app as well. MY3 is available in the Apple App Store and Google Play, free of charge. There are trained professionals available to help, 24/7. (*www.suicidepreventionlifeline.org*).

You are not alone and whatever you are going through, it's not your fault. And even if it is, it's not worth you taking your life. Everyone deserves a second chance. Give yourself permission to have that second, third or whatever chance you are on, so you can make it better for yourself first. No one is perfect. We make mistakes. Your life is so important. Think about it! You haven't been here long enough to be finished. Get the help you need so you can stay here. Even if it doesn't look like it's going to be okay right now, remember, this struggle is only temporary and this too shall pass. You will get through it. It is going to be alright! Keep in mind that we knew what happened five minutes ago, but we don't know what will happen five minutes from now! You are five minutes away from your breakthough. Therefore, giving up is **NOT** an option. It wasn't an option for me. Don't allow it to be an option for you.

You know the old saying, *"patience is a virtue"*. It is very true and relevant in the process. We have all experienced patience in one way or another. We may have had to wait in a long line at the grocery store, sit at a red light when trying to reach our destination, or we were put on hold while trying to reach someone on the telephone. However, to face serious adversity in our lives and be told that we must have patience in our given circumstances seems like an entirely different story.

Patience is to bear the inciting anger, annoyance, misfortune, delay, hardship, pain and disgrace with fortitude, calmness, and without anger, complaint or the like, at least that's what the dictionary says. Certainly, that is a tall order when you are faced with adversity and it seems like the walls are closing in on you. Patience isn't easy. Anyone who says that patience is easy to acquire, isn't being honest with themselves or they don't understand the process of patience. It was not easy for me to be patient in my situation. However, I had to learn to apply patience to my process.

Patience is acquired as you gain insight and move through life. You go through a situation that you can't rush. You don't have a thorough understanding. As you make your decisions, you have to act and wait to find out if the results will be as you had predicted.

I've learned the hard way the process of applying patience. Sometimes, you have to wait on others to do their part before you can make your move. This is not an easy task. There are times when we want people to act quickly and move at our convenience, but this is not always going to be the case. They either take their time or don't act at all. That's the frustrating part of it. What I've also learned with having patience is…I have a choice! I can choose to wait or move out on my own and accept the consequences for my actions. Most of the time, I've had to choose to do the latter. Although, these were hard decisions to make, they were valuable lessons when I was running for my life.

Having patience without complaining and remaining calm are virtues that are acquired through practice. Some people may ask, *"How are you?"* You may ask yourself, *"Does this person really care to know how I am doing?"*

It appears asking how someone is doing has become a part of casual communication instead of a serious question. We ask how someone's doing and we keep moving forward with our conversation. It is glossed over and sometimes missed. A seemingly simple conversation could go something like this:

"Hello, how are you?"

"Hi. Honestly, I'm not doing well. How are you doing?"

"Oh, that's good, I'm doing very well! You know, I was just on my way to work. Glad that we ran into each other take care. Bye!"

Have you ever been asked how you're doing and honestly said that you're actually not doing well? What happened when you told the inquiring person that you are not okay? Did they care to inquire further or did they continue on with their conversation without hearing you? It's become so simple to do this.

In my experience, I've found that when I did choose to answer honestly when I was not feeling well, I felt self-conscious because others may have felt like I was complaining. People have asked me, *"Where is your faith?"* When I was asked that, while I was going through a difficult time, it felt like they questioned my faith in God. It can be hurtful and insensitive to ask questions that seem uncaring, offensive and challenging to a person's faith.

We can avoid situations like this by being mindful of our words, and actions. We should also pay attention to how what we say and do, may affect not only our lives, but also the lives of others. Instead of questioning someone's faith, how about asking what you can do to assist them or become active and help them? If you see that someone is troubled, without them having to say it, ask…how can you help? Truthfully, calmness and patience are difficult and that is why they are virtues. Self-awareness can help us with the merit of patience.

Becoming self-aware is not something that happens overnight. Having self-awareness allows us to have the capacity for self-examination and the ability to recognize oneself as the person of whom we are, is separate from our community, government, environment and other individuals or groups. I was able to develop my self-awareness with expressing my thoughts, my emotions and paying attention to my behavior. I reached a new understanding of myself. With self-awareness, I was able to give myself true validation.

From time to time, we seek outside validation in the approval of others. We can seek validation in many different circumstances. Unfortunately, as we transform from childhood to adulthood, we haven't learned that validation is not needed. Therefore, when we don't receive it, it feels like a form a rejection.

Many victims of abuse and rape look for someone to believe their stories, which is a form of validation. If someone will believe them then they will feel better and the healing process can begin. However, because there isn't any physical evidence of the abuse and depending on the reputation of the victim, validation may be slow in coming or not at all.

When I was in the shelter, a staff member saw me laughing with the other ladies. She stopped, looked at me and said, *"how can you be laughing when your children are missing? Are you sure he's trying to kill you or are you in here because you don't want to pay your bills?"*

Everyone looked at her and then they looked at me.

I said, *"You teach a class on spirituality. You said in that class to take your burdens to the Lord and leave them there. So, if I take my burdens to the Lord and leave them there, knowing that He will answer my prayers, then why shouldn't I have a smile on my face? Why shouldn't I laugh?"*

Her response? She walked away.

I understood that I was validated by Allah when I took my first breath when I was born. I experienced freedom from needing validations by wanting to please Him. I truly believed that Allah would return my children to me at the appointed time.

I had work to do because faith without works is dead. I had to continue to do my part, so Allah could do His part, regardless of whom or what. I've learned that everyone is entitled to their feelings, their opinions and to decide what actions to take in their own life, no matter what others believe or feel! And so am I!

Today, I encourage you to start the process of believing that you don't need anyone to validate you. You have the power to create a new life, a new normal. A new way of living your life, accepting who you are and loving yourself in the process. Start today by choosing to be who you are meant to be in your higher, true-self. Believe in yourself, love yourself, and trust yourself. It all begins with you!

And in your process, don't be so hard on yourself should you slip. It's a part it. Even when you're crying, make sure you know *'why'* you're crying. Every tear is one step closer to your healing. So, cry as much as you need to. Your tears won't last long. Feel every emotion. Embrace them, accept them and then…move on. The more you resist the pain, the longer your journey will be. As you move forward, you will be creating your *"new normal"*.

MILDRED D. MUHAMMAD

CHAPTER 6

Creating a New "Normal"

What is <u>normal</u>?

It is defined as a state of being typical, of the usual or doing what is expected. To me, normal meant my family was intact. John and I were happy. Our children were healthy in mind, body and spiritually. Our business was thriving. My mother was happy and well in spite of her illnesses.

Seemingly, our lives were moving upward. We had a usual routine that worked for us. Although, we had our issues as all families do, I did not see them as issues that deeply affected our relationships with each other. At that time, I thought that we were *"normal"* because we were doing what society had expected.

In the wake of change, my eyes were open. Normal is different for everyone. Normal, for us, is not what is completely defined to the rest of world. You may find that your normal doesn't quite fit the dictionary definition of normal. In healing, we had to find a *"new normal"*.

What is a "new normal"? Well, per the Urban Dictionary, *the new normal encourages one to deal with current situations rather than lamenting what could have been.*

At one point in my life, I thought that John and I would grow old together. You know, the wedding vows that says "til death do us part". That is what I believed at one time.

My children are my life. They are the gifts that Allah has blessed me with. They are my normal.

Living without their father is now their normal. They express how much they miss him from time to time. I listen to them and comfort them and remind them of the many blessings they are surrounded with in their lives. I give them hugs, kisses and remind them that they are loved, every day. I do not analyze my children nor offer them my own opinion. If they ask for advice, I give it to them. It is normal, for me, to create a safe space for them to be able to feel what they need to feel without judgment.

A new normal, that I had to accept, is raising my children as a single parent and providing for their needs in every way that a loving mother should. Every emotion my children experience, I helped them to handle. Although they are adults now, which is new, they know I'm here for them.

I have to make sure that I take good care of myself as well. At the end of the day, I have to be sure that I am emotionally well and able to continue to care for myself and my children in a healthy way.

John, Salena, Taalibah are gifts from Allah. I am a proud mother. I was happy when I found out I was pregnant with each one. I enjoyed each pregnancy and I was happy they were born healthy. Each one has a different personality, attitude, character and love language. I took the time to learn each one and understand how they relate to each other, to me and to others. Just a great set of children I'm blessed to have.

Life took a drastic change for them in September 1999 when John moved out of our home. That was the last time we lived together as husband and wife. They experienced the different tactics John used to harass me. I tried my best to keep them from seeing how their dad was treating me. I'm not sure why I was protecting him. I should have allowed them to see him for who he was, but that would have been too painful. They were 5, 6 and 8. I'm sure our son, Lil John, was noticing the changes as the oldest child always sees more than we want them to. He became quiet, reserved and stop expressing his emotions. I was concerned about that. Our girls didn't notice much…at least I didn't think they did. They were always playing.

John was economically abusive too. We had our own auto repair service. He had access to all the funds. I only received what he gave me and when I needed something, for myself, I had to ask then justify the expense. He paid the rent and the utilities. When we lived together, he gave me $200 to purchase food for the month and I had to bring him the receipt. If I went a few cents over, I would be reprimanded for it. I had to be under $200. My mom, lived with us, and was diabetic. She needed special foods. So, I had to make $200 for food to stretch for six people monthly. And when he moved out, he gave me $50.

To keep us from going hungry, I took the experience of having little food to a spiritual level and began fasting. I'd learn to cook and fast without feeling the need to eat. My children understood what fasting meant and didn't question why I was doing it. I didn't tell my mom because I didn't want her to worry about me.

Two weeks later, I was still fasting. My mom, my children and I were seated at the dinner table. They were eating and I was drinking a cup of tea. I looked up and saw my son looking at me. He wasn't eating.

I asked, *"Honey, are you okay?"*

He said, *"Mom, you've been fasting for two weeks! You're going to be the cleanest Muslim I know!"*
I didn't know he noticed. I said, *"I know. I'm trying to receive words from God to help me with what I'm going through."*

He pushed his plate towards me and replied, *"You can have my food."*

I said, *"You, grandma and your sisters have to eat honey. I will be fine. I want you to eat your food so you can be strong."*

He said, *"Mom, you've fasted long enough. Is it Daddy? Does he give us enough money for food?"*

He was 8 years old. How did he put that together? I didn't answer. Instead, I decided to break my fast. To appease him, I took a spoonful of his food. He looked at me and smiled.

He said, *"You should feel better now."*

I said, *"I do feel better. Thank you, John."*

After that, he continued to eat his food and I continued to drink my tea.

Sadly, children can be used as pawns in some divorce cases. Especially when the relationship is abusive. I had not then nor do I now speak badly to my children about their dad. I don't believe that children should have to choose which parent to love more. They didn't ask to be here. That was a decision we made to bring our children in the world. We wanted them to make this world a better place. We strive to raise them to the best of our abilities. We wanted to be a strong family because of our children.

When things began to deteriorate within our family, John began speaking badly to our children about me by blaming me for the family splitting up.

John came over to visit our children. Salena, who was 6 years old at that time, asked him why doesn't he come home anymore.

He said, *"You can blame your mom for that. She doesn't want me here anymore."*

Salena looked at me and asked *"why"*? I told her, *"it was for the best"*. She was too young to understand the actions her dad had taken caused him to no longer be with us. Therefore, I left it at that.

The next time John came to the house; he gave our son flowers. The flowers were meant for me.

Lil John asked, *"Mommy, please let daddy come back. He's trying."*

It hurt me so to tell him no, but it hurt me worse that John would use his own son to manipulate the situation. When we were together, he never bought me flowers. I asked myself, why now? With all the abuse, economic, emotional, stalking, verbal, psychological, and spiritual, John was taking me through, he never hit me physically although each abuse felt like he did. 80% of victims don't have physical scars to prove that we are victims.

It is unfortunate that people blame the victim by making insensitive comments such as: *Well, you picked him! Why would you say such bad things about him? Why are you so thin skinned? What's wrong with you? What did you do to cause the behavior? etc.*

Such things are said without the realization that making those types of comments means you have automatically taken the side of the abuser and then you wonder why the victim doesn't speak with you anymore. If there aren't any physical scars, people just don't care. And at times, *with* physical scars, people don't care. Domestic abuse/violence has become a tolerable offense to the masses and there's no need to talk about it anymore and yet women and children are injured and dying daily.

John came over to the house. He said we needed to talk. So, we went in the garage to talk because my brother was in the house and I felt safe.

He said, *"You are not going to raise our children by yourself. You have become my enemy and as my enemy I will kill you."*

I was terrified, but I tried not to show my fear. I responded saying, *"I've been sleeping with the enemy all this time; what else are you going to do?"*

He walked rapidly towards me. I ran to my brother, who was in the kitchen. When John saw him, he left quickly.

I said to my brother, *"John is going to kill me, he's going to kill me!"*

My brother said, *"John isn't going to kill you. He's just playing."*

At that moment, my brother didn't believe me. He wasn't going to help me. I never went to my brother for help again. I asked myself, *now what am I going to do?*

Families and friends should understand that even *if* the victim returns, at that moment, you will establish yourself, in the victim's eyes, as his/her helper or supporter of the abuser. It is in that moment, that victims decide, if they will ever contact you again for help. Most family members and friends take the side of the abuser and blame the victim for the condition of the family. Most family members will threaten the victim if they report the abuser to the police leaving them without any recourse. Being cavalier about domestic violence is not the answer. Domestic violence is an epidemic, a social dis-ease. Most will deny it, but it's true.

No one had to tell me that John was not serious. He never did anything without a plan. No one listens to the victim when they should! I went to the courthouse to fill out a form requesting a restraining order. I was crying so much I could barely see the papers. I could not believe my life had spiraled into this moment. I kept thinking, *how did I get here?* I went to the phone and called Olivia. I told her what I was doing. She told me that I had to protect myself. I completed the paperwork to receive a court date.

The day of the hearing, I was scared. I went to the courthouse alone. My legs shook as I walked. I thought I might faint from fear. At all times, I stood where I could watch all the doors. I planned my escape route, just in case I saw John. I stopped crying. I was frightened, but I felt as if I was on a mission. John didn't show up.

The judge read the forms I completed. He said, *"You have to get away from this guy"*.

I said, *"Your honor, I'm trying to that."*

Thankfully, he gave me a lifetime protection order. In the protective order, visitation was included. I never tried to keep our children away from him. I honestly believe that children need both parents because they have something different to teach. He could have them anytime he wanted to be with them. Most times, victims want the father/mother to be a part of the child's life. However, the abuser takes advantage of that trust and begins to manipulate the children's emotions into thinking that the other parent doesn't love or care for them. Such a cruel thing to do to a child.

We agreed on a person who would pick up our children from me and take them to John for every other weekend visitation. From Friday morning to Sunday evening, they spent time together. Each time, I noticed changes in our children towards me. Lil John especially. We were very close and he became distant each time he returned.

It was the Friday before my Mom's birthday and Lil John had suffered an asthma attack at school. My brother went to the school to get him to bring him home. When he arrived, I had the nebulizer machine waiting for him. I called John and explained to him what happened with Lil John. I also asked him to get the girls.

After he picked them up, he called and said Tommy would be over to get Lil John. He wanted to take them to Odyssey I, an indoor family fun and game center. I was okay with that. I asked him to have them back by Sunday evening at 5:30 because we're taking Mom to Old Country Buffet on her birthday. He agreed to have them back at that time.

Just before Tommy arrived, I explained to Lil John what was happening He gave me the oddest look.

"What's wrong, honey?" I asked.

"Nothing," he said continuing to stare at me.

I said, *"Are you sure?"*

He said, *"Yes, ma'am."*

I walked out of the bedroom and went to the kitchen. I turned around and found Lil' John standing behind me, just staring.

"Honey, you know you can tell me what's bothering you, right?"

He looked like he wanted to cry, *"Yes, ma'am,"* he said.

He reached up to give me a hug. I knelt and hugged

him. He hugged me like something was wrong.

Then he said, *"I love you, Mommy."*

I said, *"I love you too, honey."*

There was something about the way he said it that concerned me. I watched him. He didn't know how to tell me what was going on inside of him. Before I could say anything else, there was a knock on the door. It was Tommy. I walked Lil John to the door. As Lil John was walking out, he looked back once more, stopped and waved.

He said, *"Bye, Mommy"*. I said, *"I'll see you later."*

The doorbell rang at 5:30 Sunday evening. I opened the door and it was Tommy, without my children. I asked, *"where are my children?"* He handed me a note. It was a hand-written note from Taalibah. Inside the note was two dollars. It read, *"happy birthday grandma. I love you, Taalibah"*.

I asked Tommy, *"What is this? Where are my children?"* He said, *"The children are with John."*

I asked him, *"What time is he bringing them home?"*

He said, *"You should call him."*

Then Tommy left and I paged John. I paged him over and over for the next couple of hours. Cellphones were not as relevant as they are now. Pagers was the way we contacted others and waited for them to call.

Finally, at 7:30, he called. However, Lil John was on the phone.

Calmly, I asked, *"What are you all doing?"*

"We're at Kmart with a list of things you asked Dad to buy," he said.

I remember giving him that list months ago, after he stopped giving money. Instead he asked me to make a list of the things the children needed.

I said, *"I thought y'all were going to Odyssey I"*.

He said, *"We are going, but we came here to pick up some things you had on the list."*

I said, *"Alright, but ask your dad when are you coming*

home."

I heard my son ask the question and I heard John say they'd be back home in an hour. I knew that it would be 8:30. Then, Lil John said, *"Mom, I love you."*

I said, *"I love you too and I'll see you later."*

Finally, 8:30 came and went. I began paging John repeatedly for the next three hours. I didn't get a call back until 11:30pm. It was John this time.

I asked him, *"When are you bringing the children back home?"*

He said, *"We're enroute from Seattle. We'll be there shortly."*

I told him okay. As I was hanging up the phone, I felt butterflies in my stomach. I felt like something was wrong. Seattle is forty-five minutes from our home in Tacoma. John had them in Seattle when I thought they were fifteen minutes away. If he could do this… I didn't want to think about what was possible.

I didn't sleep that night. I sat on the sofa waiting for the doorbell to ring. I didn't tell my mother about John's last call. She was asleep. I didn't cry; I didn't want to get upset. I was trying to be optimistic. I didn't know what John was doing but I hoped he would bring them back any minute. Still, I couldn't close my eyes without knowing where my children were.

Daylight came and time passed. First it was time for the children to wake up. Then time for them to eat. Then time for them to get dressed for school. I waited until school was open and the children had time to get there and be in their classes. I was thinking that John took them to school for me. I called the school and the secretary answered. I identified myself and asked if my children were in class. She put me on hold for a few minutes. When she came back on the phone, I felt a shiver go down my spine.

She said, *"No, Mrs. Muhammad, your children are not here. But you can call back at any time."*

I thanked her and hung up. I sat quietly. I didn't show any emotions. I didn't know what to feel, what to think or what to do.

My mom woke up. Before she said good morning, she asked about the children. I told her that I didn't know. My mother started crying.

She said, *"Why would John do that?"*

I said, *"I don't know, Mom."*

She could barely stand as I helped her to sit down. I tried to calm her. She didn't need the stress because she's diabetic. I couldn't cry or show any emotions around her. Overtime, I saw the light fading from my mothers' eyes. She was barely holding on.

I called the school every day that week. Finally, I went to the school Friday only to find out they were not there. I called the police when I returned home. They came to the house. I explained to them what occurred. They took a report and marked it *"custodial interference"*. They said since they were his children too, he had not *actually* kidnapped them. They told me that since I didn't have a parenting plan, he had just as much a right to them as I did. So, in other words, there was nothing they could do.

Someone press *'pause'* on my life. I felt empty. My children were gone. I constantly asked myself, *what am I to do?*

For the next 18 months, my struggle was trying to find my children while trying to stay alive. I needed help. I needed to find a way to get my children back but I needed to find out where they were.

Wherever he took them, he needed help to do it so someone knew where they were. *Why wouldn't they tell me? What could John have said to them, especially those who were mothers, that would keep them from telling me where my children were?* I will never understand their reasons.

I ended up leaving Tacoma, Washington in January 2001 because my mom had pneumonia. She was living in

Maryland and my sister needed my help. I didn't have my children at that time nor did I know where they were. I continued to look for them, quietly, as not to bring attention to myself for fear that if John knew where I was, he would seek me out and kill me.

It was August 31, 2001, when I received the call that my children were found and I would have to fly back to Tacoma for an emergency custody hearing.

The judge looked at the paperwork and found that I had completed my paperwork, *pro se*. Since it was in perfect order, he gave me sole custody of our children. He indicated to John that he would have to go back to court to get the order changed.

Because I filed the correct paper work, I could leave the state without letting him know where we were going and I would not be charged with kidnapping. When the case was settled, my attorney, advocate and I went into the hallway of the courthouse. John tried attacking me in the courthouse. We were able to get away and that night, I left Tacoma with my children and returned to Maryland, September 5, 2001. When I got them back, they were 8, 9 and 11. I missed 18 months of their lives. *How do I make that up? What did they see? What were they exposed to? What do I do?*

When I finally had my children with me, the *"play"* button had been pressed so I could live again. I had to study my children and they had to study me all over again. They told me they were in Antigua. Their dad told them they were going on vacation and that I was coming later. They believed him because he was their dad.

The sad news was my Mom, Olevia Green, passed December 1, 2001. Although my children talked to her, they did not get the chance to hug or kiss her. They were angry. I told them that grandma held on for a long time waiting for y'all to come back. As soon as she knew you were safe with me, she let go. Don't be angry with her. She missed y'all so much. They understood and accepted my explanation.

September 2002, the "sniper" began shooting innocent people. No one knew who it was, not even me. Someone randomly killing people was unheard of in the US. After 23 days, it turned out to be John. Law enforcement told me I was the target. They said he was killing innocent people to cover up my murder so that he could come in as the grieving father and gain custody of our children.

I had to be about the business of raising my children during a high-profile case. The news was ongoing and so were the insensitive comments. Victim-blaming for me was at an all-time high.

My focus was on my children. I protected them from hearing those comments. I tried to find a counselor. However, since it was a high-profile case, the ones that were referred to me wanted to be famous. I did not allow them with my children. The one I did find, tried to take advantage of the situation as well. So, to further protect my children, I went to the library, got a book on counseling and learned to counsel me and my children myself. I helped them to understand and compartmentalize their emotions. I set up ground rules for them to talk about their dad by creating a safe environment. This became their way of expressing themselves without feeling judged, rejected, or ashamed.

How do we move forward? How do we create a "new normal" so we can live a productive life? These were questions, and so many more, that needed answers of which I did not have. *Who was going to help us? No one stepped up before, why would they now?* I contacted victim's compensation in Maryland. They told me because I didn't have physical scars and I wasn't shot, all they could offer me was counseling…incredible!

No physical scars, no assistance. People blaming me for the innocent people killed. They thought I was a part of it. They thought I knew it was John and didn't tell the police. They didn't want to hear about the abuse me and my children suffered. It didn't matter to them. They didn't feel like I was a victim. And because they felt and some still feel this way, we didn't get the help we so badly needed. I didn't have an advocate. However, I was an advocate for my children and did my best to protect them from this kind of cruelty.

When my children reached the age of 18 and were off to college, I told each one the exact same thing. I said, *"This is where I have to let you go. Let you go to find out who you are. It is best that you go away to school so that you can make your own decisions for your life. You have to fall on your face and get up. You have to know what you will do, what you won't do and what you can't do. I'm your mother first, your friend second. I'm always here for you. When you call me, and ask for advice, I will listen to you, but you will have to make your own decisions. If you need to talk through an issue, I'm here. Understand that the final decision is always yours to make. There are consequences to each decision, whether good or bad. Be sure to think it through. I'm here to support you. I'm here to love you and to encourage you. I am proud of you and I love you."*

My son, John, attended Louisiana Tech University. He majored in Computer Information Systems. He made the football team as well. He decided he wanted to come home to begin working on his career.

My daughters, while at Suitland High School, were in the performing arts program. In that program, Mr. Boucher, their music and vocal instructor, taught the choir to sing classical music in eight different languages. They participated in competitions (local & national) and won! They sang in the combined chorus at the Inauguration Celebration at the Lincoln Memorial in 2008 for former President Barack Obama. They also participated in the combined chorus for the PBS Christmas in Washington for 4 years. And, my girls have an episode on Inside Edition. They received scholarships at the colleges they attended. Salena, attended Baldwin Wallace University majoring in vocal performance. My baby girl, Taalibah, attends Cleveland State University, majoring in vocal performance as well.

In March 2013, John, at age 23, was diagnosed with Multiple Sclerosis (MS). That diagnosis was life altering for our family. We had to learn a lot about this disease because it doesn't run in my family or John's family. I read everything trying to find out what he could and could not do. *How can we, the girls and I, help him?*

The more I read, the more I knew this was here to stay. He was constantly having relapses. The last relapse he had put him in the hospital for two months. He had become 100% disabled. He couldn't hold his head up, walk, barely talking. He was a baby all over again who needed constant care. I felt the doctors were doing nothing for him. He was dying right before my eyes and there was absolutely nothing I could do. I began praying, asking Allah what to do.

I had several speaking events during that time. Unfortunately, I had to informed the sponsors of the diagnosis with my son. And thus, I had to send all the monies back. Therefore, I could not pay my rent or other bills. I reached out for help but help didn't come. We were on the verge of being evicted and living on the streets. *How could I find another place to live while taking care of my son with no money?* He was in a wheelchair now. That was progress. But, *where would we go?* I managed to keep a few events to speak in the fall. I asked Taalibah would she please stay home from college to help me take care of John. I was so grateful she said yes. She knew I needed her help. I needed her home with him while I kept my engagements. I promised her she could return in the Spring. After a while, we had enough money to move. And I kept my promise to Taalibah as she returned to school in the Spring.

All I was thinking was that I can't lose my son. I began documenting, on Facebook, what was happening to him with my friends. I feel that I have the best friends on Facebook! They were giving me things to do, to read, to look up. Some of them have MS. They suggested other medications because the one he was on wasn't working.

Then, my Facebook friend, Dr. Valerie Gibson, sent me an inbox message. She explained how she had been reading and keeping up with my post regarding my son. She gave me her email address and we began communicating regularly. She asked me to bring my son to her office to meet a neurologist. The neurologist was her friend and she felt assured that she could help. I told John about it. He was leery because we had been through three doctors.

Dr. Valerie Gibson is a physical therapist, national speaker, and patient advocate. As owner and director of Advanced Physical Therapy and Rehabilitation Center, LLC, a private practice specializing in neurological rehabilitation, in Vienna, VA, Valerie personifies clinical excellence in neurology. Her goal is to maximize potential recovery in all aspects of neurological injury, including the general well-being of her patients.

Once we arrived, Valerie was there waiting for us. We hugged each other. I thanked her for her help and introduced her to John. He was quiet and unsure to what was to come next. We sat in the waiting room contemplating who we would see.

Soon after, we met Dr. Heidi Crayton. I didn't realize we were at her office which is the MS Center of Greater Washington located in Virginia. She is board certified with a specialty in Multiple Sclerosis. She specializes in treating black men with MS. Dr. Crayton gave John a thorough examination. I found out, through her, that the most aggressive strand of MS is in black men and it must be treated with an aggressive drug. She gave John a thorough examination and decided upon the medication that would give him his life back.

As of today, she is treating John with Tysabri. It's an infusion for one hour a month. She gave me my son back and gave him a second chance to live his life the way he was before. I will be forever grateful to Dr. Valerie and Dr.

Crayton.

John has progressed so much. He went from being 100% disabled, to be 100% able to live his life on his terms! He has his life back and is an assistant manager at Helzberg Diamonds.

My girls have established their own vocal group called *To Music;*. They have a YouTube channel http://bit.ly/2mtA7MI. They will be pursuing a career in music and I'm very proud of them. So, we have our new normal. The important part to all of this is that we are a strong family and we continue to be close.

In 2015, I had the opportunity to go back to Tacoma for a speaking engagement. While there, I met up with friends from back then to have lunch. We were happy to see each other and began sharing past and current events. One of the persons began talking about John and the situation. How terrible it was and the outcome.

She said John visited her prior to taking the children. He asked her to pray for him because he was about to do something. She said he began sweating as she prayed. When she finished, she said he got up, thanked her and left. The next thing she knew, I had called her and told her John took the children. She decided not to say anything to me about that. She said John would visit her often looking for me. She told him she didn't know where I was. John had told her the children were in Antigua.

As she was talking, I went numb. I stopped eating. For whatever reason, I couldn't say anything. Actually, it felt like someone's hand was over my mouth. I could feel the anger building, but it never came out of my mouth. I've gotten so good at hiding my emotions. However, when I returned to my hotel, I couldn't sleep.

I had an idea that a few people knew where my children were. I just didn't think that person was her. I found out that some of the people who smiled in my face, some who came to visit, knew where my children were and didn't tell me. I can only attribute my behavior to God holding my tongue to keep the peace.

Teshanne Phillip invited me to the Virgin Islands to speak at her conference. I humbly agreed to go. Teshanne is a Mother, Humanitian, Author, Ghost Writer, Motivational Speaker, Mentor, and Student in her own right. She's also a survivor of domestic violence. I asked my sister, Maisha, to go with me.

That was a bittersweet experience. Sweet because I had never been there. It is such a beautiful place. I'd never seen water that blue and clear. I was in St Thomas and St John. And the conference was great! Bitter because, I was told that Antigua is under British rule so John took our children out of the country. I was told that the living conditions of where my children were, wasn't good! When I heard that…I felt like someone stabbed me in my heart. He hated me so much that he put our children in harm's way. I cried the rest of that trip. I tried to hold it in but from time to time, tears would fall.

When I got home, I could no longer contain myself. Salena was home. I just went right up to her and held her so tightly. She asked what was wrong. I told her what I found out about Antigua and the conditions their dad had them living in. She looked at me. Then she put her head down.

I told her, *"I'm so sorry y'all went through all of that. I would have never done that to you."* I couldn't stop crying.

She started crying. She wiped my face and said, *"It's okay mom. I know."* I said, *"it's not okay Salena…it's not okay!*

She called John and Taalibah. Taalibah was in school in Ohio. John came over. He hugged me and reassured me that everything was okay.

He said, *"At one point, we lost hope. You can't work your way to be better. Wherever you are, that is where you will be for the rest of your life. You don't have to apologize, Mom. It wasn't your fault. You've done everything you can to make our lives better and you did."*

I looked at him with tears in my eyes. My heart was broken and filled with strength as I listened to his words.

He said, *"Don't cry, Mom. Please, don't cry. All we can do is keep moving forward. That's what you taught us. You have to go through your pain. And once you get through it, then we have to keep it moving, right?"*

I nodded at him. It took me a while to go through that pain. We got through it together.

My relationship with my children continues to evolve every day. They are all very smart, intelligent and wise beyond their years. They are problem solvers rather than problem dwellers.

They feel that they have been able to get through their lives as not only survivors, but also as life thrivers. They have a healthy perspective on all that they've been through. They've told me that they are grateful that I was able to help them to understand their emotions, name them and heal from them. They know that no one's opinion is more important than their own, not even mine. I taught them to meet people where they are and be patient.

To this day, they attend conferences with me. They have appeared in documentaries with me and continue to show their love and support, not only for me, but for each other.

There is an emotional connection, understanding and enlightenment when I'm working, speaking, writing and raising them.

I compartmentalized my issues regarding John, my children, law enforcement, the media, my family, friends, colleagues, associates, and even those who don't like me, so that I could get a clear picture of what was ahead of me. My mind had to be in the right place. If I did not handle it properly and with a calm spirit and sound mind, each issue would linger and healing would not be complete.

I live my life the best way that I can by knowing that my best is all I can do.

If I would have listened to the negativity surrounding me, I would not have written my books. I'm doing my best to share my story, the insight and compassion Allah has given to me.

I took charge of my life and I didn't care what other people thought or said about me. Although, others have their rights to their own opinions, I don't have to accept or internalize what people say or how they behave. I will not debate about me and my children's past. I know the truth and speak truth to help and inspire others. That is all that matters. I've found the courage to walk away from the negativity because it is my choice to exercise my right to keep peace.

I have balance in my life. Balance involves my work, my children and my faith. I have a different outlook on life. Not that I didn't take life seriously before, but being in a situation where my life and my children's lives were threatened, the experienced has caused me to take more time to appreciate the birds singing, the sun rising and setting, listening to the noises of the world and having patience in every situation. Without it, I wouldn't be healed.

Every day, I open my eyes and thank God for a new day of life. Whatever the day holds, good or bad, I am grateful. I'm grateful to be alive and to experience everything that comes with each day. I see every day as a good day. I've had some days that brought about great challenges, but at the end of the day, I remain ever grateful.

That gratefulness, spills over into my work of helping others. I allow my heart to open up to others. I keep my emotions "on" when I'm talking to those who are in need of help. There are victims who simply need someone to listen to them, believe them and help them. Some people are not sure of how to stop hurting. I've been in that place. I know how it feels. If I can help one person through their pain, then my life's work is never in vain. My purpose in life is to help others get through their trauma and make to the other side without the pain. Knowing this purpose, being aware of it, and accepting it allows me to keep striving to continue to share my story, assist others with resources, write my books and conduct one-on-one coaching. I use these tools to inspire and encourage others to step out, speak out, and have faith to accomplish every dream that is in their hearts.

My gratefulness also seeps into my faith and spirituality. My spirit soars each time I think of the goodness of Allah. God continues to bless me and my children. One of my favorite gospel songs is called *God Favors Me*. There is a verse that says: *Some days the well was dry and I have the same reply, God favors me.* That's how I feel. God favors me. I'm grateful for the blessings, anointing and favor He has and continues to bestow upon my life.

What are the steps to creating a 'new normal'? I can share what I've learned.

Creating a new normal consists of realizing that the dreams we had for our lives, did not come into fruition. We must grieve that life in our own way. We grieve the people we were. We grieve old things like our homes we've left behind, old friends we no longer talk to, businesses we've lost, and the potential of what could have been. We grieve the life we would have had. We give all of those things a proper burial, remove them from holding our spirits down, and we walk away, never looking back.

Next, sit down and look at what we desire to become now, in this *"new normal"* with new challenges and opportunities. We put our hopes and dreams down on paper and create a life that we can be proud to live. Even though there will be times things won't work out as we plan, we continue to move forward and onward in the direction we need to go to be successful. Having faith in the process, keeping God first and remembering His promises that He will restore everything that has been taken from us, helps us remain faithful and focused.

I balance my life by living in the spiritual realm. I've learned that there are three realms within the spirit. The first one is the physical realm. On this realm, fear is the controlling factor. In the physical realm, where I used to dwell, is the victim, fear, desire and anger.

I moved on to the second realm, which is the mental realm. The mental realm is also controlled by fear and love. On the mental realm, there is enlightenment and pride which are controlled by fear. There is courage and reason which is controlled by love.

Then, there is the third realm, the spiritual realm. On the spiritual realm, there is acceptance, wisdom, love and unconditional love. There is peace of mind. This is where I reside today.

Of all the realms, in which at one point or another, we all have been, the spiritual realm is where I feel the most powerful and authentic. I am optimistic about life, rather than isolated and pessimistic. Regardless of life's circumstances, I have learned to find the silver lining. Seek and ye shall find.

Finally, in creating a *new normal*, wake up in expectancy. Regardless of what it looks like in the physical realm, if we keep our faith that everything we ask for will be given, then we stand on that. Speak, whatever you desire, into existence as if were so. In the Holy Quran, it says, *"Allah will grant you your heart's desire"*. Don't say, "Lord, please help me!" Instead, say, "Lord, thank you for...." Even though you don't have it yet, you are thanking Him because you know it is coming. Trust in Him.

I know, with assurance, that I will receive what I ask for. I live in the spiritual realm. This is where I dwell. This is how I have come to where I am today. Here, to help you and others who are reading this. I am confident that I will receive all that I ask because that is the promise God has given me. He is never too early nor too late. He works at the appointed time and He works through people.

You may wonder why I am confident. I was shown and saw it with my own eyes. When my children were missing, there were many people who knew where my children were and they did not tell me. I asked Allah to protect them and keep my babies safe. In my spirit, I knew, deep in the essence of my soul, that I would get my children back. I didn't know when or where I would be. I only knew that they would come home. I never gave up. I never doubted. Even when others tried to discourage me by telling me to snap out of it, let it go and move on, I refused to give up.

Every time I look at my children, they remind me that the promises of God are true. I know He will be with me and will never leave me or my children. With faith, we live in the spiritual realm. *This is our new normal.* We were ready to heal and move forward.

CHAPTER 7

Healing & Moving Forward

My mother was the example of faith for me. She told me, when I was in my teens, to read the Psalms 20 when you are going to a meeting or you will be in the company of others. The first sentence of the scripture reads, *"May the Lord answer you when you are in distress"*. That was truly my situation for a very long time. I knew Allah would answer my prayers. I didn't doubt nor did I waiver regarding my healing or the return of my children.

My heart was broken, but I did not lose hope. The day I realized my children were gone, I walked into the living room and stood in the middle of the floor. I raised my hands and with tears in my eyes. I said, *"Oh Allah, this situation is bigger than me, John and our children. All I ask is that you protect my children and keep them safe from harm, seen and unseen. And give me the strength to handle this situation in a manner pleasing only to you"*. After I prayed, I fell to my knees and continued to cry.

I didn't know when my children would return, I just knew they would. I didn't entertain any conversations, from anyone, who spoke any doubt about whether or not my children would return. As soon as someone tried, they never heard from me again. I had to protect my mind and my spirit from any negativity that others may say or do around me. My circle became very small. That was one thing I didn't tolerate.

My focus was on learning what I needed to do to stay

positive, alive and find my children. If you weren't with me, then you were against me and you had to go. That's how tough I had to be.

There are many external influences that could have kept me from looking inward to move forward.

The good part about that is that I didn't smoke, drink or use drugs. Those factors were not a necessity for me. I decided to go inward and practice my faith to remain focused on my situation. I studied those in scripture that was close to my situation.

I studied Jacob because his son, Joseph, was missing. I studied Hagar because she was running to and fro, between the mountains, looking for help as she carried her son and no one helped her. There were those who knew where my children were, all the way in Antigua, and didn't tell me. That still boggles my mind. They watched me suffer in anguish about the location of my children.

One morning July 20, 2000, while I was in the shelter, I was saying my morning prayer. I lay out on my prayer rug and cried for two hours. I got up, rested on my knees and raised my hands while saying, "*Lord, I'm giving my children to you. I have to release them to you so I can live. I have to save myself because this pain is so deep. I know they are under the same Sun that I am. Oh Allah, please allow them to feel my love for them. Please don't let them forget my voice, my hugs, my kisses. And at the appointed time, bring them back to me. You said I have not because I ask not. I'm asking Lord and now I will remain patient. I trust and believe you know what you're doing. And I know you will bring them back to me. Ameen*".

On August 31, 2001, I received the call that law enforcement found my children. On September 5, 2001, I went back to Tacoma, Washington, for an emergency custody hearing and was granted full custody of my children. That day, Allah answered my prayer.

My prayer, my sacrifice, my life and my death are all

for Allah, the Lord of the Worlds. I prayed, aloud, "*I love you Allah and thank you for loving me. Please don't turn away from me for surely, I would be one of the losers!*"

Having faith allowed me to appreciate what it means to stay focused. Staying focused is seeing what is ahead of you and not dwelling on what happened in your past. You can remember these things, but you must not let them weigh you down. Instead, learn and grow from your experiences in order to gain wisdom.

Staying focused is also paying attention when other situations present themselves. Sometimes they can come right after another, creating a feeling of being overwhelmed. At times, we may want to give up because we feel like there is no relief. Relief comes when we continue to work on our goals and they come into fruition. When the situation becomes too overwhelming, break it down to the least common denominator, then handle it piece by piece. This will give you a feeling of accomplishment and a determination to keep going.

Writing down your goals, going over your ideas in your mind and working can help you to maintain your focus. This is what I have done over the years and it works for me and my family.

Everyone must find what works for them. You must learn what works for you in a positive way. What may work for one person may not be the best for another person. There are many ways to maintain focus. There is painting, exercising, sports, writing, dancing, public speaking, therapy, etc. The possibilities are endless! The point is to find what positively works for you and stick with it.

Parents with children who have suffered trauma, often wonder how can they help their children to move forward on their well-being. I struggled with this in the beginning after our isolation. I've learned that talking to children is a helpful way. Create a safe space for them. Encourage them to talk about what they've experienced in the safe environment you've created. That is the first step to opening the lines of communication and starting a healthy dialogue with your children. Simply, ask your children how are they doing.

Don't probe or poke at them when you ask questions. Instead, listen to them. Then pick something that you noticed your child is struggling with and make it a productive, positive conversation by acknowledging their concerns. This helps them to feel safe and know that you care about what they have to say and how they feel.

Stay focused on positive things and moving forward, as you speak what you desire into existence. Again, speak, out loud, about the lifestyle that you desire, as if it were so, and keep it in the forefront of your mind. Keep your eye on your goals until you have achieved them. Continue to create new goals while teaching your children to do the same. Lead by example and your children will follow.

Other ways that have helped me to stay in tune with my healing are: *listening to inspirational music, reading devotional quotes, writing down and reciting affirmations and reading scriptures from the Holy Quran and Bible.* My faith plays a great part in helping me to stay focused.

Another way to healing and moving forward is to stop listening to naysayers. Naysayers are people who consistently express negative or pessimistic views even in the face of disagreement to their negativity. They are there to bring you down and discourage you from moving forward. Their role is to cast a dim light of doom into the light of people who seek peace and positivity in their lives.

How do you defeat them? By strategically moving away from them, having faith in the process, exercising faith and setting boundaries. Setting and maintaining boundaries are important for your wellness and peace of mind.

You can set boundaries for yourself by knowing and stating what you will do, what you can't do and what you won't do. Let your yes mean yes and your no mean no! Keep your word. It builds integrity. Make sure your words and actions line up. This applies to every relationship you have in your life, whether it is a relationship with family, co-workers, friends, lovers, spouse, acquaintances, etc.

For your good health, you must set and maintain boundaries in every relationship. Also, it is important to set boundaries for yourself. Know what your limits are and do not stretch beyond those limits until you have grown and gained insight.

Setting boundaries serves as a protection for yourself and your family. It helps you to be in touch with yourself to maintain sanity and control of your emotions. When you can maintain yourself, you are able to help others, including your loved ones.

To love others, you must first love yourself. To love yourself means you know and understand that you are a valuable person. You are aware that you are valuable enough to share your love with others. As you share your love, you will not allow others to take advantage of you, even while you are caring for someone else. Ephesians 2 says God created us to be a Masterpiece. *Do you walk in that?*

There are times when you won't notice when others are trying to take advantage of you. However, when you do take notice, you have two choices. You can allow the relationship to continue or let the relationship to go. Think it through and decide.

Sometimes, to love yourself means to let go of issues and people that have hindered your growth. *If you must let go, do so.* Let go of the negativity you feel towards yourself. Never speak defeat over your life. Words are powerful. If you are saying, I will never heal. Guess what? You won't. Love yourself enough to only speak positive affirmations over your life. When releasing people from your life, take inventory of the relationship and decide what is in YOUR best interest.

It works the same for loving someone else. If you love someone, love with an open hand. Never love anything or anyone more than you love yourself. You are just as important as anyone else. And if you don't take of yourself, no one else will.

It is important to love yourself because if you don't, your love for others will not be built on a healthy foundation. If that is the case, it can't be ignored and must be addressed.

We can live to survive. However, there is a difference in being a survivor and being a thriver. A survivor is a person who has lived through any kind of trauma, tragedy, life altering experience or disaster. A thriver is someone who was once a survivor and they *choose* to use their experiences to educate others in their healing and recovery. To help others, we must be able to have boundaries, maintain them and have love.

In my journey, I have the honor of meeting many people who are on their journey to recovery from trauma. I listen to their stories and I share insight from my experiences. Some people are in so much pain, they come to me in despair and in need of a listening ear.

A thriver is someone who can maintain who they are and help others who are in need without it negatively affecting them. That is going beyond surviving in your life. It requires love, patience and understanding, with yourself, to get this far in life.

Love applies to healing the spirit as it helps us to move forward. Love heals us and replenishes us in ways that we are not aware of until we've moved away from the pain. Love moves us forward.

Moving forward simply means to push ahead even though we look backwards. *What is the point of looking back when your whole life is ahead of you?* Think of driving. The rear-view mirror is so small. There's nothing that needs your attention. That's your past. The front windshield is an example of the vast opportunities and challenges that need your attention. You are moving forward. You decide if the direction you are going will be positive or negative.

I've learned that looking back can have good and bad

consequences. Some people live in their past because the present may seem too painful to face. The past reminds them of a more simpler and happier time. When you're stuck in your past, you constantly talk about the *"good ole days"*, so that they can relive, in memory, how their lives were. It can be difficult to let go of the past. However, we should not think about the past so much that we forget to live in the present.

There is nothing wrong with reflecting on the past as long as it is a brief time of reflection and then we should keep moving forward. When you allow the struggles of life to stop you from moving forward, depression can set in and grip you so hard that it seems like your troubles are too hard to overcome. Despite what you are going through, try to keep moving forward as the motion will help you understand who you are and how you should do your best to live your life to the fullest.

When you try to ignore the past, you can stunt your spiritual growth. Some people allow shame, guilt or anger to keep them from facing the past. The level of trauma that has occurred in a person's past will determine the difficulty factor in facing the pain. Some people can handle it on their own while others need the assistance of a counselor. Don't be afraid to reach out for help. Counseling can work! If you find yourself stuck in the past and unable to move forward you should seek help. Find a counselor that resonates with your spirit because that person will be the most effective in assisting you with working through the trauma, healing and eventually your recovery. And even though you have a counselor, life coach, or therapist, have your own agenda. *What is it you need help with?* Explain what you need and be pro-active in your recovery.

You don't have to feel ashamed of seeking help for what has happened to you. Talking it out will help you to see your situation clearer. Sometimes we can block our own blessings because we are not looking at the situation the way that we should. Other people, whom you trust, can see what you cannot see. People who care about you, will listen to you and help you see what it is that you need to see.

Getting help from a professional can help you come to terms with what has happened. It is important to be honest with yourself because it prevents you from stumbling through your life. Sometimes, we don't want to face the truth within ourselves, and be in the moment to feel what we need to feel. We would rather ignore it and hope that it goes away. However, life does not work that way if we want to move forward. When we ignore it, we end up standing in our own way and we allow the issue to get out of control.

When you stand in your way, you are not accepting the changes that are occurring in your life. You end up fighting yourself to make a decision and in the process, time is moving and your growth stops. Separate your emotions from the actual facts. Once you can accept the changes and understand them, you realize the decision was long overdue and it's time to move on.

For me and my children, moving forward was the only way that we could survive. I had to assist my children on a journey from the past to the present by making sure they understood, adjusted and accepted the painful reality we were living. I used age appropriate language and set up emotional boundaries so that we would not emotionally injure themselves or each other. I needed them to be emotionally balanced children so that they could grow into emotionally healthy adults. It is a lot easier to raise your children to be well-balanced. There are so many people in pain.

As time passed, I saw the growth in my children. I saw the positive change because the process worked. They were able to respond to questions without feeling ashamed or guilty. They spoke openly and learned to articulate their feelings and emotions.

To overcome, you must understand what happened to you emotionally, psychologically, physically, spiritually, and in some cases, financially. Even though you and others in your life were affected, you are only responsible for how you react. Your reaction reflects who you are.

You had to go through what has transpired so that you can get to where you are today and where you're meant to be in the future. The trials that we face positions us for something greater, that's what I believe. You don't have to glorify it. Embrace your past, learn the lessons and gain wisdom so that you are not destined to repeat it.

The good thing about remembering the past, and not pushing it away or ignoring it, is to look at how much you have grown. How much wisdom have you gained throughout the years? How far have you come? These are wise questions to ask yourself when reflecting on your past. The answers to these questions, depending on how honest you are with yourself, can help you to move forward.

The result of moving forward is enjoying the rewards from the work that you had put forth in the past as it comes to fruition. Moving forward should not be looked upon as a setback in difficult times. Understanding that it is a process, will allow you to continue to look towards your future.

Scripture says we should reflect on the good things the Lord has done. Your faith can be renewed! When bad times come around, know that God is with you. For me, this fact brings comfort, strength, insight and guidance through my present situation. I know that I've been through the most difficult challenge in my life. Everything that comes along now, is easy. Therefore, I do not fear the future. I've been pushed to my extreme limits and I survived. With my faith, I feel that I can make it through anything by the Grace of God.

For me, God is the very essence of who I am. I love Allah first and foremost, then myself, my children and everything else follows. Those are the boundaries that have been set. *God always comes first.* I am happy that Allah has healed my heart and it is no longer broken. And by His Grace & Mercy, ***I am Still Standing***.

MILDRED D. MUHAMMAD

AFTERWORD

My purpose in life keeps me moving forward every day. Helping others confront, understand and move on from their emotional trauma is what I've come to learn to do best, next to being a good mother. I tell my story openly to participants at conferences. My work is rewarding for me. It is a blessing to be able to help people every day of my life. I find that when I serve my purpose, my energy is at its highest because I'm doing what God has put me here to do.

The most important lesson to be learned from my story is that ___*you don't have to have physical scars to be a victim of domestic abuse/violence.*___ Do not ignore someone if they say that they are being abused. It doesn't matter if you see the scars or not, each situation should be taken seriously.

I once was under incredible stress while my children and I were suffering. The help I needed was slow in coming because no one believed me. It was important for me and my children to learn that the abuse was not our fault. There were some people who tried to make us feel like what was happening was my fault. I had to find people who believed me and who would continue to support me. I've learned not to take no as a final answer when looking for help. If a person tells me no, I find another way and I keep striving until I get the results and answers that I seek.

Whether someone assists you or not, if you seek change in your life, you will find a way to make that change happen. Sometimes, to make a major change we must push forward, not dwell on the past, gain insight and forgive.

If you are no longer in an abusive relationship, you may think about and miss your abuser. That is normal and part of the process. Don't beat yourself up for that. Cry as much as you need to, then think! Don't just think about the good times. Balance your thinking and include the bad times too. Keep a proper perspective on the relationship and you will get through it. Don't go back to what God delivered you from.

There are times, when you are not aware, that an abusive relationship has begun. You've met an abuser but you're introduced to their *representative'*. The person you met and fell in love with? Yeah, that was an illusion. A *'character'* created to lure you into their web of lies. The representative stayed around long enough to secure that emotional attachment. The representative watched you tell your friends and family you met someone different from anyone else. Everything you'd been looking for. You took this person around family and friends which secured his/or her position in your life. Once the attachment was secured, the abuser feels the confidence to slowly make his/her entrance.

The abuse began with a verbal assault by calling you out of your name or something was said to hurt your spirit. You know the line was crossed but it caught you off guard. You began making excuses or blaming yourself. You didn't know it wasn't your fault! You began to doubt everything about yourself as well as your judgment. The abuse escalated into emotional, psychological, stalking, economic, spiritual. Guilt and shame began to set in. You couldn't tell anyone about the abuse because you feel stupid. *How could you not see?* You couldn't see because you weren't supposed to! It's that simple.

Some say there had to be signs. They don't know how clever your abuser is. You told everyone this is the person of your dreams. *How can you go back and tell them you are being abused?* Now you feel beaten down and trapped. You feel like a caged bird. Your wings have been clipped and you can no longer fly.

For some, a physical altercation began and worsened over time. Once the physical assaults begin, your abuser has no regard for your life. It is now easy to kill you.

Now you're thinking, who can I tell? What should I do? Who will believe me? *What can you do?* Be strategic and tell someone. Not just anyone...**one trust friend!** Expose the abuser. Abuse grows in silence. Don't take on emotions that are not yours. Your abuser transferred his/her guilt and shame onto you. Those emotions are not your burdens to carry. Release yourself from feeling you are stupid, unloved, should have seen it coming, too intelligent to be a victim, you picked him/her...stop accepting those negative comments from yourself and others. Be very strategic when you are planning your escape. I've written a safety plan. Its listed in the back of this book.

Tell only one person what you are planning to do. If you tell more than one person, you risk the abuser finding out and all your planning will be for nothing. Don't put your plans on social media. You don't know all your abusers' friends. Just because your abuser doesn't have access to your social media, doesn't mean you are not being watched and reported on.

You may say, I don't know if I'm in an abusive relationship. Every relationship has its problems and you're right. So, do this. Get a sheet of paper. Draw a line down the middle. Mark one column 'Pros' and the other 'Cons'. You are analyzing the RELATIONSHIP not the person. We all have flaws and fall short.

Separate your emotions from the actual facts. For this exercise to work properly, do this alone. You have to be completely honest. As you write in each column, don't make excuses for the behavior. Look at it for what it is. You are not responsible for someone else's behavior. Everyone is accountable for themselves. This may take a while and a few pages. However, once you have completed the list, read over it.

If the pros outweigh the cons, you can look at the cons and work on them to make the relationship better. However, if the cons outweigh the pros, you have a decision to make. Whether you chose to stay or leave, it is your decision to make. Think it through and chose wisely.

You may know someone who is in an abusive relationship and you don't know what to do. I do not advocate for anyone to put themselves in harms' way trying to assist their family member or friend. And since domestic violence is an epidemic, I'm certain that we all know someone who is or was a victim. So, here's one solution you can use to assist.

First, examine your emotions and establish, with yourself, what you are prepared to do. If you are married, discuss your intentions with your spouse. They may be able to add some insight and together you can come up with a solution. Take inventory of what you will do, what you won't do and what you can't do. For example, *"Can they stay with you? Are you willing to give them money should they ask? How far are you willing to go?"* Once you've set your boundaries, take your family member or friend to lunch, not dinner because their time maybe tracked. Once you are at the restaurant, don't ask, *'what's going on'*? You already know and you're wasting time with frivolous questions. With your boundaries in place, ask this question, *"how can I help"*?

That person may look at you strange because no one has ever asked that question before. Everyone has been telling the victim what to do, instead of asking, what they want to do. You have just empowered him or her to take control of their situation. They may sit for a while and wonder what to say because they know what they need but feel curious as to why you are asking that question. If they don't answer, don't offer suggestions. You don't want to risk sounding like their abuser. Just say, *'take your time and when you are ready, just know I'm here."* Assure them that everything that is said between you two is confidential and they are safe with you. And if you are married, let them know your spouse knows and is onboard with you. You have just saved a life.

Never discuss anything in an email or in text messages. Face-to-face communication only. Never talk about the situation on the phone when the abuser or children are around. You have the element of surprise…keep it. Don't feel that you are so removed from the abuser that you don't care what happens. You have dropped your guard and lost your advantage. Be strategic, move slowly, pay attention! Your life and the lives of your children are at stake. You are at war and you need to understand that. Every move has to be thought through. Only tell one trusted friend…**ONE!**

Once you're out of the abusive relationship, resources may be difficult to find. This is one resource that I've recommended to others and it has been successful. This website, www.domesticshelters.org, has resources for each state and city. If your city is not listed, select the one closest to you. Being a survivor is not easy. Even though you are no longer in the relationship, don't let your guards down. You know your abuser better than anyone. Don't be afraid to call law enforcement.

I really know how you feel, what you're thinking and the challenges you will face. Try not to isolate yourself. When others have the desire to help you…allow them to…at your pace. Don't allow others to push you in a direction you are not willing to go. You have choices. Choose wisely!

I've learned that forgiveness is a personal choice. No one should be forced to forgive if they do not want to. Some people may feel that to forgive a person for their wrong-doing means forgetting and letting that person off the hook.

I chose to forgive John. I didn't need feedback from him or approval of my forgiveness from him. I chose to forgive him for myself and my children. I realized when I lingered on the past, it held me back from moving forward. I made the choice to release myself from John. I detached. I severed the emotional tie. The emotional charge was gone.

After I chose to forgive John for everything, my

nightmares diminished. I no longer had flash backs and I let go of my fear. I did not carry bags around with John's name on them. Not forgiving him, for me, was allowing him to maintain a level of control in my life. I had to let that baggage go. I dissected my situation to the least common denominator, dealt with it and prayed to be released from my trauma. I gave it to God and let it go. You have heard of the saying *"Let God and let go"*. It is powerful and meaningful when it comes to forgiveness. The power of forgiveness is in your hands.

To achieve my peace of mind, was a long, painful journey. Every tear was worth the trip. The ability to genuinely smile, laugh and enjoy this life, feels so good.

You may be saying to yourself, "I'll never get to that point". My response…**YES YOU CAN!** Just heal at your own pace. Don't rush through it. You may miss an emotion that needs attention and find it come up again for a different reason, in a different way. You may slip a few times…that's okay. Give yourself permission to make a mistake.

Keep in mind that you too can get to the point of living and saying, *"I'm Still Standing"*. It can happen.

I live a life of expectancy and my life continues to evolve. I'm excited about my future.

I'M STILL STANDING

MILDRED D. MUHAMMAD

About Mildred

Mildred D. Muhammad is a Globally-Awarded Recognized Keynote Speaker, International Expert Speaker for the US

 Dept. of State, Certified Consultant w/Office on Victims of Crime, CNN Contributor, Domestic Abuse Survivor, Certified Domestic Violence Advocate, Life Coach, Author, Trainer & Educator traveling and speaking on a national and international platform to discuss her life of terror, abuse and heartache, all while promoting Domestic Abuse/Violence Awareness and Prevention.

As the ex-wife of the D.C. sniper, John A. Muhammad, who went on a three-week rampage, with the end result, as stated by law enforcement, was to find Mildred and kill her too, the very personal details of her experiences involving fear, abuse and many of times, victim-blaming, has allowed Mildred's mission to be even more influential and of greater purpose. Simply stated, she was a victim who became a survivor and is now a warrior on the issues of domestic abuse/violence. She shares her expertise on what it's like to be a victim and a survivor of domestic violence *"without physical scars"* to various conferences, seminars, workshop audiences which include victims and survivors of domestic violence, advocates, law enforcement professionals, therapists, counselors, mental and medical health providers, university and college students as well as conduct military personnel training regarding domestic violence. Her authenticity is as remarkable as her unforgettable story of abuse. She explains the perils of PTSD (*post-traumatic stress disorder*) soldiers suffer when returning from a war zone as well as victims who are diagnosed with PTSD.

After counseling herself and her children to survive victim-blaming through the midst of adversity, she transformed her tragic circumstances into an opportunity to establish ground on all forms of Domestic Violence that are often overlooked such as verbal, mental, economic, spiritual, stalking and emotional abuse. With more vocation and not only speaking of the details and the realities of Domestic Violence, Mildred makes it her mission to be a vessel of support and healing to all those affected by Domestic Abuse/Violence.

Her critically acclaimed memoir, *Scared Silent: When the One You Love Becomes the One You Fear,* was published by Simon & Schuster in 2009. Muhammad has self-published two working journals, *"A Survivor's Journal" & "Dare to Heal"*, as well as *"Planning My Escape" (a comprehensive step by-step safety plan)* specifically for victims and survivors to help with the emotions that others may not understand and strategically leaving an abusive relationship.

She has received many awards such a Special Commendation presented by the US Dept of Justice, Office on Violence Against Women, Maya Angelou "Still I Rise" Award, Shirley Chisholm Woman of Courage Award and REDBOOK Strength & Spirit HEROES Award, as well as multiple awards and Commendations from the military community, Certificates of Recognition for her ongoing work with victims and survivors of domestic violence.

Mildred Muhammad has appeared in the following TV shows: *Lifetime Movie Network Series, "Monster in My*

Family"; CNN documentary, "The Minds of the Sniper"; TruTV documentary "The DC Sniper's Wife" produced by award-winning producer, Barbara Kopple; Discovery Channel, "Who The Bleep Did I Marry"; Investigation Channel Series, "Escaped ~ The Sniper's Wife: Episode 2; MSNBC documentary, 'I Married The Beltway Sniper" and the syndicated TV show, Crime Watch Daily.

Mildred Muhammad has been interviewed on *Oprah: Where Are They Now, Anderson, Ricki Lake, Katie Couric, Issues with Jane Velez Mitchell, The Mike Huckabee Show,* TruTV's *In Session, Larry King Live, The Tyra Banks Show,* and *Good Morning America,* and has appeared on BET and other local and national TV interviews. She has also been interviewed by various national and international radio shows, internet radio, various national and international newspapers, and internet blogs and magazines worldwide, including the *BBC, NPR, Essence, Jet, The Washington Post,* and *Newsweek.*

For more information or to book Mildred Muhammad
for your event, visit her website,
www.MildredMuhammad.com.

Follow Mildred:

https://www.facebook.com/MildredDMuhammad/

https://twitter.com/mildredmuhammad

MILDRED D. MUHAMMAD

Mildred

John   Salena   Taalibah

Montgomery College – Rockville Campus
Domestic Violence Program
Rockville, Maryland

YWCA Pierce County Domestic Violence Luncheon
Strengthening, Healing & Empowering Ourselves After Trauma
Tacoma, Washington

Willow Domestic Violence Center Conference
Rochester, NY

1ˢᵗ Annual Sole to Soul Walk
Sable House
Dallas, OR

Military Awards and Commendations

*NAS Oceana Fleet & Family Support Domestic Violence Training
Virginia Beach, VA*

Florida Coalition Against Domestic Violence Conference
Orlando, FL

Jackson State University
Fifteenth Annual Mississippi Child Welfare Institute Conference ~
Dept. of Social Work
Jackson, MS

Other books available from Mildred

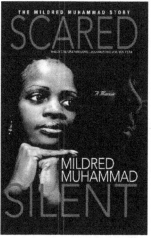

Scared Silent: When the one you love, becomes the one you fear

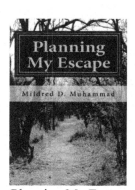

A Survivor's Journal   Planning My Escape   Dare to Heal

Get your autographed copies:
www.MildredMuhammad.com

Made in the USA
Coppell, TX
17 October 2022

84770160R00075